Budgeting and Performance Management in the Public Sector

Public sector management and accounting scholarship has witnessed enormous change over the last four decades. Several reform paradigms have become well-known and disseminated worldwide, under acronyms such as NPM (New Public Management), NPG (New Public Governance), and PV (Public Value). At the start of a new decade, questions arise as to what will come next. This book reviews and investigates the key components of NPM, NPG, and PV, and discusses what lies beyond these acronyms. It analyzes the claimed benefits and drawbacks of each of the three paradigms, using reviews of the pertinent literature, as well as a raft of case studies. The integration of theoretical and empirical insights contributes to a better understanding of what has changed and what has remained the same over the years.

Specifically, this book stands out in its use of performance measurement and budgetary lenses to explore the multidimensional processes of reform and change in the public sector. By focusing on the crucially important transformations that have occurred in the field, reviewing several paradigms, and analyzing different practices from a longitudinal and comparative perspective, the book will be useful in guiding students and scholars of public management and accounting.

Sara Giovanna Mauro is currently a Post-Doctoral Research Fellow at the Institute of Management, Scuola Superiore Sant'Anna, Pisa, Italy. She has also studied and researched abroad (University College Cork, Ireland; New Jersey Institute of Technology, USA; Tampere University, Finland; Kristianstad University, Sweden). Her main research interests are in public sector budgeting and performance measurement and management.

Routledge Focus on Accounting and Auditing

Advances in the fields of accounting and auditing as areas of research and education, alongside shifts in the global economy, present a constantly shifting environment. This presents challenges for scholars and practitioners trying to keep up with the latest important insights in both theory and professional practice. Routledge Focus on Accounting and Auditing presents concise texts on key topics in the world of accounting research.

Individually, each title in the series provides coverage of a key topic in accounting and auditing, whilst collectively, the series forms a comprehensive collection across the discipline of accounting.

Gender and Corporate Governance
Francisco Bravo-Urquiza and Nuria Reguera-Alvarado

Accounting, Representation and Responsibility
Deleuze and Guattarí Perspectives
Niels Joseph Lennon

Public Sector Audit
David C. Hay and Carolyn J. Cordery

Integrated Reporting and Corporate Governance
Boards, Long-Term Value Creation, and the New Accountability
Laura Girella

Budgeting and Performance Management in the Public Sector
Sara Giovanna Mauro

For more information about this series, please visit: www.routledge.com/Routledge-Focus-on-Accounting-and-Auditing/book-series/RFAA

Budgeting and Performance Management in the Public Sector

Sara Giovanna Mauro

Routledge
Taylor & Francis Group

LONDON AND NEW YORK

First published 2021
by Routledge
2 Park Square, Milton Park, Abingdon, Oxon OX14 4RN

and by Routledge
605 Third Avenue, New York, NY 10158

Routledge is an imprint of the Taylor & Francis Group, an Informa business

© 2021 Sara Giovanna Mauro

British Library Cataloguing-in-Publication Data
A catalogue record for this book is available from the British Library

Library of Congress Cataloging-in-Publication Data
Names: Mauro, Sara Giovanna, author.
Title: Budgeting and performance management in the public sector / Sara Giovanna Mauro.
Description: Abingdon, Oxon ; New York, NY : Routledge, 2022. | Series: Routledge focus on accounting and auditing | Includes bibliographical references and index.
Identifiers: LCCN 2021006559 (print) | LCCN 2021006560 (ebook)
Subjects: LCSH: Budget. | Budget process. | Performance--Management. | Public administration.
Classification: LCC HJ2009 .M29 2022 (print) | LCC HJ2009 (ebook) | DDC 352.4/8--dc23
LC record available at https://lccn.loc.gov/2021006559
LC ebook record available at https://lccn.loc.gov/2021006560

ISBN: 978-0-367-56167-3 (hbk)
ISBN: 978-0-367-56174-1 (pbk)
ISBN: 978-1-003-09670-2 (ebk)

Typeset in Times New Roman
by Deanta Global Publishing Services, Chennai, India

Contents

List of illustrations

Figures

Tables

Boxes

Acknowledgement

This book is the result of a long journey that began with my PhD. It has been made possible thanks to many colleagues with whom I have shared the journey and who have contributed to enrich it with their precious insights, ideas and feedbacks.

In particular, I would like to thank Professors Cinquini Lino and Grossi Giuseppe for their constant support, continuous mentoring and valuable teachings along the way.

I am also grateful to Routledge editorial staff for their precious assistance, in particular to Kristina Abbotts and Christiana Mandizha for their support throughout the development of this project. Further, I would like to thank the reviewers of this book proposal for their precious suggestions and constructive feedback. They have been generous in sharing their experience and knowledge.

And last but not least, my thanks go to Tommaso and my family for their constant presence and trustful encouragement.

Introduction

Reform paradigms in the public sector: In the quest for what?

In an era of continuous reforms, there have been attempts at reinventing the government (Osborne and Gaebler 1992) and shifting and redesigning the relationships between politicians-managers and state-citizens. Further, traditional public values have been challenged by private values and the boundaries of public sector organizations have become blurred. Several factors are responsible for these changes. Among others, budget deficits, financial crises, globalization, digitalization, and pandemics have shocked the public sector over previous decades. Economic, political, and societal pressures have been continuously redefining public needs and expectations. With the beginning of a new decade that is characterized by new economic shocks and societal changes, questions regarding what comes next arise naturally.

The process of public sector reform has been the subject of study and debate from public administration, public sector management, and accounting perspectives. According to the academic debate, one source for change in public sector organizations has been represented by administrative paradigms (Polzer et al. 2016), such as New Public Management (NPM), New Public Governance (NPG), and Public Value (PV). These paradigms have become well known and are popular worldwide, most commonly referred to by their acronyms, and have inspired and guided the introduction of multiple practices in public sector organizations. Although paradigms and reform trajectories can provide an approximate and simplified representation of different scenarios across countries, they are also useful in explaining reform trends in the public sector and reflect on underlying belief systems.

The present book aims at reviewing and investigating the key components of NPM, NPG, and PV and goes beyond the mere use of these acronyms. The book intends to analyze and discuss the claimed benefits and drawbacks of each of the paradigms, utilizing reviews of pertinent literature and case studies.

NPM and NPG have been leading approaches in the public sector over the last several decades. They are dominant reform paradigms that aim to address the challenges of the traditional Weberian-style public administration. The old model of public administration, labelled the traditional bureaucracy or ancien régime (Hughes 1998; Pollitt and Bouckaert 2011), is the result of the classical public administration (Wilson 1887) and Weberian bureaucratic principles. The most recurrent features of this paradigm are the separation of politics and administration, hierarchical command, centralized bureaucracy, central planning, and compliance with rules. This model has been criticized (e.g. Osborne and Gaebler 1992) for being unsuitable to address the evolving challenges of public sector organizations and this has paved the way for new reform trajectories.

NPM was developed in the 1980s (Hood 1991, 1995) to introduce a managerial approach for governing the public sector. NPM is a 'loose term' that encompasses multiple concepts and tools (Hood 1991, 3). It is a complex and innovative mix of old and new reforms inspired by several theoretical perspectives, from the public choice theory to management theory as well as from the classical and neo-classical public administration theory to the principal-agent theory (Gruening 2001). Although it is characterized by numerous concepts and cross-country differences, it has a 'claim to universality' that can be identified in its major components (Hood 1991), which are built around the redefinition of the boundaries of government (e.g. privatization), the reshaping of the structure of the public sector (e.g. decentralization), and the adoption of a managerial approach by focusing on results. This shift from a focus on input to a focus on results has led to an 'increase in the amount of information and change in the type of information generated and used for budgeting and management purposes' (Kristensen et al. 2002, 10). This result orientation represents an undisputed and relevant component of NPM. Indeed, a set of managerial and institutional reforms has gradually been introduced to make the public sector more business-like, broadening the perspective on performance measurement and performance information (Jansen 2008). Consequently, several criticisms have been raised, particularly by those who state that the gap between the public and private sectors increases the likelihood of employing symbolic managerial practices in the public field (Lapsley 1999). Therefore, NPM has been criticized for its poor implementation (Arnaboldi et al. 2015) and has lost ground over the years, according to some scholars (Dunleavy et al. 2006; Lynn 1998). Nevertheless, NPM-oriented reforms remain on the agenda of public sector organizations (Dan and Pollitt 2015; Hood and Peters 2004; de Vries and Nemec 2013), and it can be said that NPM is still alive.

In response to the criticisms of NPM and, simultaneously, as a means of meeting new needs, other approaches have attracted the attention of scholars and practitioners. A well-developed reform movement that was considered the 'shadow of the future' (Osborne 2006, 381) is the NPG, which emphasizes an inter-organizational perspective through collaboration among public, private, and mixed public–private organizations. NPG acknowledges the existence of a pluralist state with multiple possible arrangements of the delivery of public services beyond the government-market alternative, as networks between governments, businesses, and non-profit organizations (Klijn and Koppenjan 2015; Osborne 2010). This paradigm exemplifies the ongoing redefinition of the boundaries of the public sector and emphasizes the need for a shift from a focus on public sector organizations to a focus on public services.

In this vein, the concept of public value, as elaborated by Moore in 1995 in his book *Creating Public Value*, has emphasized the final aim of the managerial work of public sector organizations in terms of (delivery of public services), paving the way to the paradigm of PV. Although it has been questioned whether it can be considered a proper paradigm or not, it is here assimilated to a paradigm (O'Flynn 2007; Stoker 2006) linked to the founding elements of NPM. PV focuses on the ultimate goal of creating value for society by delivering public services and highlights the relevance of accounting for public value creation. However, as with NPM, the paradigms of NPG and PV have also been contested and discussed. For example, PV has enlivened a debate among scholars who have attempted to cope with the challenging definition and measurement of *public value* and the consequent gap between its theory and practice (Guthrie and Russo 2014). Despite criticisms and drawbacks, these paradigms remain inspiring public sector reforms.

The objectives of this book are to illustrate and discuss these main paradigms that have influenced public management and accounting from the 1980s onwards, providing both theoretical and empirical insights and comparing some of the major changes that have occurred in budgeting and performance measurement as effects of these paradigms. Hence, through a review of extant literature and an analysis of empirical cases, the book can synthesize different reform paradigms and their (expected) impacts on public sector organizations and public services.

This book investigates the three paradigms (NPM, NPG, and PV), recognizing the different perspectives on them. In particular, the book recognizes the different interpretations of the three paradigms as alternative or simultaneous approaches. On the one hand, scholars have interpreted them as distinct and alternative. In this vein, NPM has been interpreted as a transitory state from the traditional model of public administration to more recent models (Dunleavy and Hood 1994; Osborne 2010); moreover, it has been claimed to be 'dead', replaced by digital-era governance (Dunleavy et al. 2006). According to another perspective, it has been recognized that different paradigms can co-exist in a dialectical manner. Public organizations become increasingly complex and hybrid because of the combination of elements from different paradigms, as old public administration, NPM, and post-NPM (Christensen 2012). One position on hybridization states that hybrid organizations are those that combine elements of different *logics*, where the institutional concept of logics can refer to the different paradigms. Elements of the different paradigms can be integrated. According to some scholars, their integration is exemplified in the paradigm of the Neo-Weberian State that mixes and integrates core ideas from multiple paradigms, as Weberian-style public administration, and NPM (Pollitt and Bouckaert 2011). Accordingly, it is possible to state that each new paradigm inevitably builds on the previous ones, being influenced by them and incorporating a few of their elements (e.g. Hyndman et al. 2014; Liguori 2012).

A focus on budget and performance

The three reform paradigms of NPM, NPG, and PV are the objects of theoretical and empirical investigation in the next chapters. The integration of theoretical and empirical insights can contribute to a better understanding of what has changed and what has remained the same over the years. Specifically, this book stands out in terms of its use of performance measurement, performance management, and budgetary lenses to investigate the multidimensional processes of reform and changes in the public sector.

Although performance is not a new issue that public organizations are required to deal with and the improvement of performance is an old desire, the interpretation of performance has changed significantly with the advent of NPM. Consequently, performance measurement and management systems have been adopted to define, measure, monitor, and manage performance. However, the conceptualization and management of performance have not remained stable over time. On the contrary, the concept of performance has been redefined over time to reflect the changes ongoing in the public sector and the measurement of performance has been required to take into account new forms of service delivery and to cope with the changes in the governance of public sector organizations inspired, for instance, by the NPG. The performance measurement and management systems have impacted and are still impacting public sector organizations and are thus considered an important dimension of analysis.

Among others, the orientation to performance has also influenced public budgeting. Budgeting has always played a central role in public organizations, but its features and roles have been redefined over time and still need to be discussed (Anessi-Pessina et al. 2016). According to Wildavsky (1961), 'The budget is the life-blood of the government, the financial reflection of what the government does or intends to do' (184). This poses significant challenges, considering that public budgeting is central in the life of governments and a complex phenomenon involving multiple stakeholders, powers, interests, and values (Rubin 2019; Schick 1966; Wildavsky 1961). The public budget has traditionally been intended to function as a financial plan that serves multiple purposes. First, it is used to plan the expected pattern of income and expenditure; then, it is employed to control the use of resources and, in addition, can serve as a communication tool and policy document (de Vries et al. 2019). The process whereby the public budget is formed and allocations are planned has been reformed over time, and the different functions of the budget have received varying amounts of attention. NPM has reinforced the influence of performance information in public budgeting, moving beyond traditional approaches. More recently, in an attempt to modernize public budgeting and meet the changing needs of society, a growing emphasis has been placed on (1) the role of the different actors in the budgeting process, especially the role of citizens, as made evident by the revitalization of participatory budgeting, and (2) the final goal of delivering public value through the use of public resources, as shown by the so-called public value budgeting. In this regard, the influence of NPG and PV has been crucial. This book looks at the changes in public budgeting in light of the main paradigms discussed here.

Organization of the book

The rest of the book is organized into several chapters.

Chapter 1 focuses on the illustration of the NPM paradigm and discusses its key components, claimed benefits, and critical aspects, as brought out in academic debate on the subject. Although NPM is well known, this chapter is useful to identify and focus the attention on key issues that will be further analyzed in the remainder of the book and compared to other paradigms. Accordingly, this chapter sets the ground for the second chapter, where the theoretical analysis of NPM is complemented by the empirical investigation of key practices adopted in the spirit of this paradigm.

Chapter 2 is empirical in its nature and focuses on the rational orientation towards measuring performance and utilizing performance information in the decision-making process. It begins with an analysis of the performance measurement and management system by supporting the theoretical discussion of its key components and challenges through insights into a field as controversial as higher education. The chapter proceeds with an analysis of the use of performance information in the decision-making process and specifically in budgetary decision-making. This is known, among other names, as performance-based budgeting (PBB). The practice is introduced, described, and discussed in light of its long history. The main theoretical approaches to PBB are explained in order to indicate why and how this old practice can remain alive. Thereafter, several experiences with PBB undertaken by countries with different practices in the field (Italy, Finland, Sweden, Germany, and the Netherlands) are discussed to shed light on the differentiation of PBB.

Chapter 3 introduces the other paradigms of NPG and PV. This chapter illustrates the key components and criticalities of these paradigms and provides an overview of these reform movements, which can be considered partially as successors of NPM and in part as parallel reforms. This chapter sets the ground for the fourth chapter, where the theoretical analysis of paradigms, and specifically of the NPG, is complemented by the empirical investigation of key practices adopted accordingly.

Chapter 4 provides insights into empirical experiences, as co-production practices and participatory budgeting, which are characterized by new relationships between state and citizens, new approaches to public service delivery, and a greater focus on effectiveness and outcome improvement. These reforms are first described and explained and then discussed through the illustration of empirical cases. These experiences are suitable for shedding light and reflecting on the changes undertaken by performance management and budgeting as a result of the development of new paradigms.

The final chapter draws the conclusions of the book, recalling and summarizing what has been discussed in the previous chapters. In particular, the chapter reflects on the 'evolution' or 'co-existence' or 'co-development' of multiple paradigms, such as NPM, NPG, and PV, in light of the practices they have inspired. The chapter provides final reflections on the changes undertaken by budgeting and performance in the public sector on the basis of the practices previously illustrated and reviewed.

References

Anessi-Pessina, E., Barbera, C., Sicilia, M., and Steccolini, I. 2016. "Public sector budgeting: A European review of accounting and public management journals." *Accounting, Auditing & Accountability Journal* 29, 3: 491–519.
Arnaboldi, M., Lapsley, I., and Steccolini, I. 2015. "Performance management in the public sector: The ultimate challenge." *Financial Accountability & Management* 31, 1: 1–22.
Christensen, T. 2012. "Post-NPM and changing public governance." *Journal of Political Science & Economics* 1, 1: 1–11.

Dan, S., and Pollitt, C. 2015. "NPM can work: An optimistic review of the impact of new public management reforms in central and eastern Europe." *Public Management Review* 17, 9: 1305–1332.

Dunleavy, P., and Hood, C. 1994. "From old public administration to new public management." *Public Money & Management* 14, 3: 9–16.

Dunleavy, P., Margetts, H., Bastow, S., and Tinkler, J. 2006. "New public management is dead: Long live digital-era governance." *Journal of Public Administration Research & Theory* 16, 3: 467–494.

Gruening, G. 2001. "Origin and theoretical basis of new public management." *International Public Management Journal* 4, 1: 1–25.

Guthrie, J., and Russo, S. 2014. "Public value management: Challenge of defining, measuring and reporting for public services." In *Public Value Management, Measurement and Reporting*, edited by Guthrie, J., Marcon, G., Russo, S., Farneti, F., 3–17. Emerald Group Publishing Limited.

Hood, C. 1991. "A public management for all seasons?." *Public Administration* 69, 1: 3–19.

Hood, C. 1995. "The 'new public management' in the 1980s: Variations on a theme." *Accounting, Organizations & Society* 20, 2–3: 93–109.

Hood, C., and Peters, G. 2004. "The middle aging of new public management: Into the age of paradox?." *Journal of Public Administration Research & Theory* 14, 3: 267–282.

Hughes, O. E. 1998. "The traditional model of public administration". In *Public Management and Administration*, edited by Hughes, O. E., 22–51. Palgrave.

Hyndman, N., Liguori, M., Meyer, R.E., Polzer, T., Rota, S., and Seiwald, J. 2014. "The translation and sedimentation of accounting reforms. A comparison of the UK, Austrian and Italian experiences." *Critical Perspectives on Accounting* 25, 4–5: 388–408.

Jansen, E.P. 2008. "New public management: Perspectives on performance and the use of performance information." *Financial Accountability & Management* 24, 2: 169–191.

Klijn, E.H., and Koppenjan, J. 2015. *Governance Networks in the Public Sector.* Routledge.

Kristensen, J.K., Groszyk, W., and Bühler, B. 2002. "Outcome-focused management and budgeting." *OECD Journal on Budgeting* 1, 4: 7–34.

Lapsley, I. 1999. "Accounting and the new public management: Instruments of substantive efficiency or a rationalising modernity?." *Financial Accountability & Management* 15, 3-4: 201–207.

Liguori, M. 2012. "Radical change, accounting and public sector reforms: A comparison of Italian and Canadian municipalities." *Financial Accountability & Management* 28, 4: 437–463.

Lynn Jr, L.E. 1998. "The new public management: How to transform a theme into a legacy." *Public Administration Review* 58, 3: 231–237.

Moore, M.H. (1995). *Creating Public Value: Strategic Management in Government.* Harvard University Press.

O'Flynn, J. 2007. "From new public management to public value: Paradigmatic change and managerial implications." *Australian Journal of Public Administration* 66, 3: 353–366.

Osborne, S.P. 2006. "The new public governance?" *Public Management Review* 8, 3: 377–387.

Osborne, S.P. 2010. "Introduction the (new) public governance: A suitable case for treatment?." In *The New Public Governance?*, edited by Osborne, S.P., 17–32. Routledge.

Osborne, D., and Gaebler, T. 1992. *Reinventing Government: How the Entrepreneurial Spirit is Transforming the Public Sector*. Perseus Books.

Pollitt, C., and Bouckaert, G. 2011. *Public Management Reform: A Comparative Analysis of NPM, the Neo-Weberian State, and New Public Governance*. Oxford University Press.

Polzer, T., Meyer, R.E., Höllerer, M.A., and Seiwald, J. 2016. "Institutional hybridity in public sector reform: Replacement, blending, or layering of administrative paradigms". In *How Institutions Matter!*, edited by Gehman, J., Lounsbury, M., and Greenwood, R., 69–99. Emerald Group Publishing Limited.

Rubin, I.S. 2019. *The Politics of Public Budgeting: Getting and Spending, Borrowing and Balancing*. CQ Press.

Schick, A. 1966. "The road to PPB: The stages of budget reform." *Public Administration Review* 26, 4: 243–258.

Stoker, G. 2006. "Public value management: A new narrative for networked governance?" *American Review of Public Administration* 36, 1: 41–57.

De Vries, M., and Nemec, J. 2013. "Public sector reform: An overview of recent literature and research on NPM and alternative paths." *International Journal of Public Sector Management* 26, 1: 4–16.

De Vries, M., Nemec, J., and Špaček, D. 2019. *Performance-Based Budgeting in the Public Sector*. Palgrave Macmillan.

Wildavsky, A. 1961. "Political implications of budgetary reform." *Public Administration Review* 21, 4: 183–190.

Wilson, W. 1887. "The study of administration." *Political Science Quarterly* 2, 2: 197–222.

1 New Public Management and its heritage

1.1 The heritage of NPM: Performance meanings and practices

1.1.1 NPM: What is beyond the acronym?

NPM, which stands for New Public Management, is the label attached to a set of ideas which had become a reform package designed to transform public bureaucracies to improve public service efficiency and effectiveness and introduce flexibility. The 'loose term' of NPM (Hood 1991, 3) has been coined to represent and group the reforms adopted by public sector organizations since the 1980s. In the United States, those significant changes in the public sector were marked in the book *Reinventing Government* by Osborne and Gaebler in 1992, which became a reference point for those interested in reforming public sector organizations.

NPM has been inspired by multiple theoretical perspectives. Institutional perspectives and the principal–agent theory have, over time, confirmed the most popular approaches used to analyze NPM reforms (Talbot 2010; van de Walle and Groeneveld 2016), but several other perspectives, such as public choice theory, management theory, classical public administration, neoclassical public administration, property rights theory, and transaction-cost economics (Gruening 2001; O'Flynn 2007), have influenced NPM. These theoretical approaches differ and may contribute to explain the different elements of NPM. For instance, the principal–agent theory is evident in the NPM elements concerning the separation between purchasers and providers of services and the establishment of contractual relationships to deliver service, while the public choice theory is evident in the emphasis put on private sector provision (O'Flynn 2007).

This variety of theoretical approaches beyond NPM has stimulated the emergence of different ideas and reforms that are usually grouped under the NPM label, partially being the source for the variation of these reforms across countries. Further, the variation in how NPM is adopted and implemented across countries can be ascribed to the different politico-administrative regimes which influence the choice of the reforms and their feasibility (Pollitt and Bouckaert 2011). Accordingly, it is possible to distinguish between countries more open to NPM ideas, the Anglo-Saxon countries, and those less open to it, such as the continental European states of Belgium, France, Germany, and Italy. Apart from the differences across contexts, a 'claim to universality' (Hood 1991, 8) exists and can be detected in the key components of the paradigm (see Box 1.1).

BOX 1.1: THE ELEMENTS OF NPM

According to Hood (1991), the doctrinal components of NPM can be summarized in the following manner:

1. Hands-on professional management
2. Explicit standards and measures of performance
3. Greater emphasis on output controls
4. Shift to disaggregation of units in the public sector
5. Shift to greater competition in the public sector
6. Emphasis on private sector styles of management practice
7. Emphasis on greater discipline and parsimony in resource use

---

The NPM reform movement assumes that private sector management frameworks and practices can be employed to improve the efficiency and effectiveness of the public sector (Stiglitz 1989). Therefore, NPM can be said to introduce managerialism in public governments, which is visible in the emphasis placed on performance. Public sector organizations are expected to work under 'competition' within a 'market', thereby being forced to control their outputs and improve their performance. According to a neo-liberal approach, the private sector represents the best and only means to good performance. In this vein, the NPM movement introduces institutional reforms that are designed to increase decentralization and externalization. Decentralization implies the transfer of responsibilities and tasks among levels of governments, referring in particular to the delegation of activities away from the central government. The redefinition of roles and tasks is determined by the need of increasing efficiency and effectiveness in the delivery of public services. Externalization refers to the transfer of responsibilities and tasks outside of government, assigning activities to other organizations different from public administrations. In such a context, the government's role shifts from one of producer (rowing) to one of regulator (steering), and managers are recognized as having additional flexibility and responsibility to manage.

In the spirit of NPM, there is high trust in the market and this leads to identifying in private sector actors those suitable for delivering public services. This calls for measuring and controlling the activities of public organizations through accounting techniques (Hood 1995). The need for controlling these activities has created an audit explosion to the extent that society assumes the traits of an 'audit society' (Power 1997), where financial and non-financial dimensions are checked and audited. A cultural shift towards quantification and control over results has led to what has been defined as 'accountingization' (Power and Laughlin 1992). This implies a new means of interpreting accountability, whereby accounting plays an instrumental role and becomes visible to the extent that accounting information significantly shapes how certain systems should work (Kurunmaki et al. 2003). Public sector accounting is recognized as the key tool to make the public sector quantifiable and managerial (Lapsley 2009; Olson et al. 1998). This may suggest that the advent of NPM has represented a golden age for public sector accounting research (Steccolini 2019), supporting its growth. The significant role played by accounting-based financial management techniques has led to consider financial management as a key technical component of NPM (Olson et al. 1998).

Taking into account the previous different issues, the label of NPM is indicated to be an inclusive term which embraces ideas regarding the need to reinvent the government by making it results-oriented, customer driven, and competitive (Osborne and Gaebler 1992). The reforms inspired by NPM are hence concerned with different dimensions of public sector organizations, such as their structure, governance systems, human resource management, and finance and accounting systems (see Table 1.1 for a few examples). An important accounting issue in the public domain concerns the budgeting process, which has been the object of specific reforms in the spirit of NPM, as will be discussed in the next chapter (see Box 1.2 for an overview of public budget).

Table 1.1 NPM reforms

Governance	People	Accounting and auditing
• Separation of politics and administration • Decentralization • Outsourcing • Privatization • Agencification	• Freedom to manage • Professional management (incentives) • Performance pay	• Accrual accounting • Performance budgeting • Performance audit • Accountability for results

BOX 1.2: WHAT IS PUBLIC BUDGET?

A *public budget* can be intended as a plan expressed in quantitative (monetary) terms (Budding et al. 2015), whereby public sector organizations define the resources to be used in a given period for realizing certain programmes by forecasting revenues and expenditures for that period. In Rubin's (2010) view, 'Public budgets describe what governments do by listing how they spend money' (1).

The process whereby a budget is made is defined as *budgeting*. This term can be used to indicate the entire budgeting cycle, referring to when the budget is formulated and approved, and also to its execution and reporting (Saliterer et al. 2017). The budgeting cycle hence includes several phases, such as budget formulation, approval, execution, and auditing.

There are multiple functions that a public budget fulfils throughout its cycle, and these have been classified and labelled differently by scholars over time. For instance, they can be classified as follows (Budding et al. 2015):

1. Planning function
2. Control function
3. Coordination and communication functions
4. Motivation function

Similarly, they can be grouped into the following (Schick 1966):

1. Planning function
2. Management function
3. Control function

The planning function is of primary importance and concerns the definition of objectives and programmes, the allocation of resources, and their subsequent authorization. The allocation of (limited) resources implies choices among alternatives, and this is the essence of budgeting (Rubin 2010). The old question of 'On what basis shall it be decided to allocate X dollars to activity A instead of activity B?' (Key 1940, 1138) is still at the heart of budgeting theory in the search for a mechanism whereby allocative decisions can be made. In fulfilling this function, the political nature of the public budget clearly emerges since allocative decisions are influenced by political priorities, stakeholders' preferences, and power positions. Consequently, the budget represents the plan that should guide public organizations' activities, and the budget allocations reflect the priorities over which negotiations among various actors have been incurred. As a planning tool, the budget is oriented towards the future, and the time horizon is traditionally one year but it may be even longer (Mussari 2017). The management function concerns the execution of the budget and the control function concerns the oversight of the use of resources. Public budgets need to be real and accurate since, in principle, all spending must be within the limits indicated in the budget (de Vries et al. 2019). This underlines the technical nature of this document. By setting the budget, politicians authorize responsible politicians or managers to spend a certain amount of money on specified items/ activities (Budding et al. 2015). Accordingly, the budget becomes an authorizing document, which is used as a control tool to guarantee that resources are spent consistently within the budget. The budget can also be used to assign objectives to managers and make them accountable for the results achieved. It can then be employed to communicate the results to the legislature and external stakeholders by addressing accountability requirements. In this regard, the managerial nature of a budget emerges more clearly with its use as a tool to make managers accountable for the use of public resources and the achievement of results. Therefore, the budget can be used to coordinate the relevant activities, communicate the goals to be achieved and resources to be used, and motivate managers by setting targets linked to performance evaluations.

In light of this set of different functions and the multidimensional nature of a budget as a technical, political, and managerial tool, it is possible to affirm that the public budget (and budgeting) is built on negotiations among different actors (Wildavsky 1964). Both politicians and managers are required to carefully reflect on and discuss the resources to be spent and the goals to be achieved. Several participants with different priorities, interests, and power take part in these negotiations, and in this context, the role of citizens and their preferences are pivotal since the elected officials are making decisions on how to use citizens' money. Therefore, the established understanding of a public budget and budgeting is strongly determined by the underlying politics of public budgeting (Rubin 2010), which concerns how decisions are made and implemented, and is influenced by the interactions and negations among multiple actors.

The different budget functions discussed above are not mutually exclusive, although they have not received the same amount of attention or been assigned the same relevance over time (Anessi-Pessina et al. 2016). Specifically, the planning–management–control balance can change (Schick 1966). Over time, budget formats and processes have been continuously revised to find an efficient and effective answer to Key's question of the 'best way' to allocate resources. This process demonstrates the changing relevance of the different functions of a budget. Specifically, the development of different budgeting processes – such as incremental budgeting, programme budgeting, performance-based budgeting, and participatory budgeting – demonstrates the different emphasis of each function over time. The prevalence of one function over another influences the formats and processes of a budget and results in budgeting reforms, as shown, for instance, by the shift from incremental budgeting in the traditional public administration model to programme budgeting in the post-war expansion period which can be considered a planning-oriented tool, to a revitalization of performance budgeting in the spirit of NPM which can be considered a management-oriented tool (Saliterer et al. 2017; Schick 1966).

1.1.2 Performance meanings and practices

A key concept of the managerial innovations introduced in the public sector is *performance*. Performance is not an innovative term and, not surprisingly, the desire to improve performance is not new (Curristine 2005; Hoskin and Macve 1986). The concept of performance improvement preceded the development of NPM and will continue to exist (Kettl and Kelman 2007). Nevertheless, although specific themes and devices have characterized each wave of reform, performance has remained a permanent feature in public sector reforms (Talbot 2005) and has been closely related to NPM.

Performance is a multidimensional and multifaceted concept, employed with different meanings and for different purposes. Performance is considered as a 'buzzword' or even 'the great unknown' (Pollitt and Bouckaert 2011; van Dooren et al. 2010). Over time, the conceptualization of what performance precisely refers to has changed.

According to the traditional public administration paradigm, performance is determined by compliance with rules and regulations. Spending resources within set limits was one of the main objectives of public sector organizations and the key parameter to assess performance. The focus on inputs and the control of processes were key in the performance measurement systems used by public sector organizations. The drawback of this approach is that there is limited consideration of how resources are used and whether the final objectives are achieved. Thus, the inefficiency and ineffectiveness of the system became evident and relevant, thereby calling for a shift from the control of input to the measurement of outputs. New systems that were able to cope with the more complex and challenging tasks faced by administrations and with the pressures for efficiency were required. Governments began facing expenditure constraints and were thus obliged to pay more attention to the use of the limited available resources (Curristine 2005). In this new context, NPM has found opportunities to flourish and has paved the way for the advance of performance movements emphasizing the measurement of government performance and the development of a performance agenda (van Dooren et al. 2010), built on initiatives oriented to measuring performance.

The interpretation of performance has thus undergone a significant transformation. It has been often considered as the result of a production process in which inputs are allocated to produce outputs and generate outcomes (see Box 1.3). The linkages between these different elements are measured in terms of economy, efficiency, and effectiveness – the well-known 3E model. Successively, a fourth E – equity – has been added to indicate the equal opportunity of everybody to access a public service (Bouckaert and Van Doren 2003). Performance measures, indicators, and targets are set accordingly to measure the efficiency in the use of resources (link between inputs and outputs) and the effectiveness of the services delivered (link between output and outcome), which implies the consideration of the ability to satisfy citizens' needs. In this vein, an input/output model is considered and calculated with reference to a single unit of analysis (organization), and performance usually refers to the results of the activities realized according to the expected objectives that need to be attained. Thus, measuring performance has the overall goal of improving it – that is, strengthening the degree to which governments can fulfil their goals (Behn 2003).

BOX 1.3: A VIEW OF PERFORMANCE

Among the different perspectives adopted to interpret and define the concept of performance, the following alternatives can be identified:

1. Performance as a production, where tasks are intentionally carried out by performing actors
2. Performance as a competence or capacity, when the focus is on the quality of the actions carried out

3. Performance as results, when the focus is on the quality of the achievements
4. Performance as sustainable results, when the focus is on the quality of both actions and achievements

A widely accepted interpretation of performance focuses on the concept as the result of a production process, following a production logic proper for the private sector (Pollitt and Bouckaert 2004). The underlying idea is that public sector organizations provide products and services, and their performance can be measured according to how this production process works and which results are produced. This entails a judgement of the quality of actions and results, which represents one of the key reasons why conceptualizing and then measuring performance in the public sector are challenging.

A further complication is represented by the link between performance and value. If performance is considered as the realization of values or it is assessed against values as reference framework, this implies that many different concepts, such as equity, fairness, and extensiveness, should be taken into account.

Source: Van Dooren, Bouckaert, and Halligan 2010

Despite the widespread adoption of this perspective, the interpretation and understanding of performance remain challenging issues. The 'conceptual space' of performance is still under debate and to be properly defined, six distinctions can be taken into account in the public sector (Andersen et al. 2016): Identity of stakeholders (politicians, users, or professionals), formality (implicit or explicit) and subjectivity of measures (perceptions or more objective measures), type of process or product focus (fair process, user's participation, effectiveness, quantity, etc.), and unit of analysis (organization, individual, etc.). The variation in how these distinctions are defined contributes to the different delineation and measurement of performance.

The set of activities designed to quantify performance can be grouped under the label of performance measurement, one of the most resilient aspects of NPM reforms (Modell 2004). The measurement of performance has become a distinct trait of NPM (Modell 2004; van Helden et al. 2008). Under NPM, quantitative information is introduced on a government-wide scale and in all management functions (van Dooren 2008). Therefore, the myth of quantification has created an industry of performance measurement (Modell 2004). Performance has been measured at different levels (Bouckaert and Halligan 2008) or foci (Talbot 2005) – at the macro level (government-wide performance), the meso level (policy sector, a network, or a chain of events), and the micro-level (individual organizations). Further, traditionally the performance of public servants has also been measured and assessed.

The rationalist approach that has inspired the measurement of performance prescribes a proper 'performance cycle' according to which the measurement of performance should be followed by the management of performance, broadly defined by the Organisation for Economic Co-operation and Development (OECD) as the set of 'corporate management, performance information, evaluation, performance monitoring, assessment and performance reporting' (Curristine 2005, 131). Performance management has attracted substantial attention and has, thus, become a part of modern governance arrangements (Pollitt and Bouckaert 2004), representing a priority in the agenda of numerous public sector organizations. Performance management requires that performance measures are elaborated and discussed in order to produce information that could be used by organizations to inform their decision-making. The adoption and design of performance measures are crucial for the success of the performance cycle. However, what makes the difference in the end is represented by the 'use' dimension, a key step of this rationalist and textbook performance cycle. Indeed, in order to assess the success or failure of a performance initiative, it is essential to study how performance information is utilized (van Dooren 2008), without which actual performance management cannot occur (Vakkuri 2010). Therefore, performance management becomes the necessary prerequisite for practices aimed at employing performance information in the decision-making process in public sector organizations.

There are many uses for performance information and different purposes for which performance information is utilized (Behn 2003; Talbot 2005). One approach recognizes that the functions of measuring performance are the creation of transparency, learning, appraising, and sanctioning (de Bruijn 2007). Accordingly, performance measurement is expected to increase transparency by providing evidence of the results achieved and reinforcing accountability. Consequently, these pieces of information may be used to understand and learn what works and what can be improved. On this basis, it is possible to appraise the performance of an organization and eventually provide positive or negative sanctions. In a broader view, according to Behn (2003), performance measures can be used to evaluate, control, budget, motivate, promote, celebrate, learn, and improve. Among these managerial purposes, the improvement of performance is considered as the final overall goal.

The extent to which performance information can be utilized depends on its type and the users, as has been demonstrated in an extant literature review on performance management (van Helden and Reichard 2016). The utilization of performance information is less formalized compared to performance reporting; thus the former is more difficult to investigate. Substantial research has focused on the issue of measuring performance and, broadly, managing it. More recently, scholars have investigated the production and misuse of performance information and have paid specific attention to how it is utilized by both politicians and managers (e.g. Grossi et al. 2016; Kroll 2015; Liguori et al. 2012; Moynihan and Pandey 2010; Saliterer and Korac 2013; Taylor 2009; ter Bogt 2004). The results of these academic studies indicate the difficulties in utilizing performance information, thereby contributing to the debate on the limitations of NPM.

1.2 The rise and decline of NPM: A 'golden age and cage'

It is difficult to comprehensively assess NPM reforms especially if the goals are subject to interpretation and changes, and final appraisals are then ambiguous (Skelley 2002). However, the feasibility and usefulness of NPM have been the object of great scrutiny and debate.

NPM has been severely criticized because of its poor and limited implementation and because of its inability to attain expected goals (Lapsley 2009; Lynn 1998). The transfer of private tools and practices in the public sector has often failed to produce the expected initial outcomes, thereby resulting in unintentional outcomes (Ashraf and Uddin 2016; Dunleavy et al. 2006; Hood and Peters 2004; Tambulasi 2009). Thus, there are numerous controversial and unexpected effects of NPM and different views can be identified in this regard, with one view mainly focused on the value dimension and another view focused on the components and contextual variables of reforms (Mauro et al. 2019).

The first view concerns the value dimension. Previous studies have contested the unsuitability of NPM principles for the public sector as a reason for the negative results of its reforms. Scholars have critically emphasized how a managerial approach in the public sector can lead to controversial results. Private sector logics may result in the diffusion of the entrepreneurial ethos (Morales et al. 2014) that transforms the public servant into a new *homo oeconomicus* (Hoskin 2015). These critiques have been supported by empirical studies that reveal the tension between different values derived from the introduction of NPM reforms (Kartalis et al. 2016): The excessive focus on results and business-related values may undermine the commitment to key public values (Broadbent et al. 2001; Lorenz 2012). An excessive focus on measurement may distract from the delivery of public services and the creation of value.

Another view focuses on the mismatch between the inherent features of NPM reforms and contextual factors of public sector organizations. Critiques have focused on the challenges which have occurred in the process of reform implementation. They discuss the limitations and structural features of the public sector context as a source for poor implementation of NPM reforms. There are a wide range of possible reasons for the poor and partial implementation of NPM reforms, ranging from state incapacity, little political support, lack of debate on reforms, inappropriate design of reforms, limited technical competencies, and professional authority (ter Bogt et al. 2015; Lorenz 2012; Sarker 2006). Hence, the failure in meeting the initial expectations can be due to a lack of fit between the original design of a reform and the specific context in which it has been employed. This is evident, for example, in the limited use of performance information (Sterck 2007) or in the increase in administrative controls rather than an improvement in governance (Christensen and Laegreid 2001). The new requirements in terms of performance measurement and management may create new administrative burdens rather than simplifying procedures and making them more focused on service delivery. Performance and performance measurement have been defined as classic 'wicked problems' since performance has multiple implications and the actors involved may interpret it differently (de Vries et al. 2019). Indeed, performance information and instruments are inherently ambiguous since there is no unique interpretation of performance; public sector organizations may have ambiguous goals to attain and the rational intentions for improving performance may lead to bounded rational and managerial practices (Moynihan 2015; Vakkuri 2010). In this vein, performance measurement and management systems have revealed, in practice, the numerous paradoxes to which they are linked (van Thiel and Leeuw 2002). The 'performance paradox' has been defined as the weak correlation between performance indicators and performance itself since what is reported can be better or worse than reported (van Thiel and Leeuw 2002). One of the most relevant and frequent factors contributing to a partial representation of performance lies in the limited measurement of the most significant dimension of performance – the outcome; this is because it is also the most difficult to measure and tends to be ignored (Almqvist 2001).

Determining whether or not NPM works remains an unresolved concern (Mauro et al. 2019). Researchers hold that NPM died along with the end of neo-liberalism (Dunleavy et al. 2006; Lynn 1998). The failures of NPM reforms have contributed to building this view, according to which the movement poses more questions than answers (Lynn 1998). On the contrary, an alternative thesis supports the idea that NPM is still alive (De Vries and Nemec 2013; Hyndman and Lapsley 2016). Prior studies have recognized the existence of limits and paradoxes in the reforms inspired by NPM but have considered them to be inevitable, thereby supporting the thesis that NPM may still be worth the effort, and its success may depend on the administrative capacity and the existence of a 'fitting context' (Dan and Pollitt 2015; Hood and Peters 2004). Indeed, although more recent paradigms are becoming increasingly widespread, a recent review of the literature on NPM (de Vries and Nemec 2013) demonstrates that the ideas of NPM are still reflected in different tools. Performance measures, controls on the achievement of objectives – for example, in terms of performance audit – contracting, outsourcing, the disaggregation of and competition within the public sector, and the emphasis on the quality of service delivery are examples of NPM devices that are still on the agenda of public sector organizations. Despite the drawbacks and criticisms, it cannot be denied that the key components of NPM are evident in the practices of public sector organizations.

To conclude, a third potential alternative can be identified. Indeed, even if key components of NPM are still adopted by public sector organizations, it may be opportune to revise NPM in light of the current situation in which public sector organizations are expected to perform. This is partially reflected in the fact that, although a claim for universality can be detected in the identification of common elements in NPM reforms across countries, the movement has been characterized by a significant local variation (Hammerschmid and Meyer 2005). NPM has been and continues to be an international phenomenon but with local variations (Hyndman et al. 2014). In addition, and in particular, NPM may not be the only paradigm in place. The process of change does not follow a linear path and multiple paradigms can indeed coexist (Hyndman et al. 2014; Liguori 2012). Even if the NPM reform movement has been considered a golden age for public sector accounting since it has flourished in the spirit of NPM and accountingization, NPM may become a cage which makes it relevant to evade in order to identify new paradigms that are adequate in the current times (Steccolini 2019).

References

Almqvist R. 2001. "'Management by contract': A study of programmatic and technological aspects." *Public Administration* 79, 3: 689–706.
Andersen, L.B., Boesen, A., and Pedersen, L.H., 2016. "Performance in public organizations: Clarifying the conceptual space." *Public Administration Review* 76, 6: 852–862.
Anessi-Pessina, E., Barbera, C., Sicilia, M., and Steccolini, I., 2016. Public sector budgeting: A European review of accounting and public management journals. *Accounting, Auditing & Accountability Journal* 29, 3: 491–519.

Ashraf, J., and Uddin, S. 2016. "New public management, cost savings and regressive effects: A case from a less developed country." *Critical Perspectives on Accounting* 41: 18–33.

Behn, R.D. 2003. "Why measure performance? Different purposes require different measures." *Public Administration Review* 63, 5: 586–606.

ter Bogt, H.J. 2004. "Politicians in search of performance information?-Survey research on Dutch Aldermen's use of performance information." *Financial Accountability & Management* 20, 3: 221–252.

ter Bogt, H.J., Helden, G.J., and Kolk, B. 2015. "Challenging the NPM ideas about performance management: Selectivity and differentiation in outcome-oriented performance budgeting." *Financial Accountability & Management* 31, 3: 287–315.

Bouckaert, G., and van Doren, W. 2003. "Performance measurement and management in public sector organisations". In *Public Management and Governance*, edited by Bovaird, T. and Lofler, E., 151–164. Routledge.

Bouckaert, G., and Halligan, J. 2008. "Comparing performance across public sectors." In *Performance Information in the Public Sector*, edited by Van Dooren, W. and Van de Walle, S., 72–93. Palgrave Macmillan.

Broadbent, J., Jacobs, K., and Laughlin, R. 2001. "Organisational resistance strategies to unwanted accounting and finance changes: The case of general medical practice in the UK." *Accounting, Auditing & Accountability Journal* 14, 5: 565–586.

De Bruijn, H., 2007. *Managing Performance in the Public Sector*. Routledge.

Budding, T., Grossi, G., and Tagesson, T. 2015. *Public Sector Accounting*. Routledge.

Christensen, T., and Laegreid, P. 2001. "New public management: The effects of contractualism and devolution on political control." *Public Management Review* 3, 1: 73–94.

Curristine, T. 2005. "Government performance: Lessons and challenges." *OECD Journal on Budgeting* 5, 1: 127–151.

Dan, S., and Pollitt, C. 2015. "NPM can work: An optimistic review of the impact of new public management reforms in central and eastern Europe." *Public Management Review* 17, 9: 1305–1332.

Van Dooren, W. 2008. "Nothing new under the sun? Change and continuity in the twentieth-century performance movements." In *Performance Information in the Public Sector*, edited by Van Dooren, W. and Van de Walle, S., 11–23. Palgrave Macmillan.

Van Dooren, W., Bouckaert, G., and Halligan, J. 2010. *Performance Management in the Public Sector*. Routledge.

Dunleavy, P., Margetts, H., Bastow, S., and Tinkler, J. 2006. "New public management is dead: Long live digital-era governance." *Journal of Public Administration Research & Theory* 16, 3: 467–494.

Grossi, G., Reichard, C., and Ruggiero, P. 2016. "Appropriateness and use of performance information in the budgeting process: Some experiences from German and Italian municipalities." *Public Performance & Management Review* 39, 3: 581–606.

Gruening, G. 2001. "Origin and theoretical basis of New Public Management." *International Public Management Journal* 4, 1: 1–25.

Hammerschmid, G., and Meyer, R.E. 2005. "New public management in Austria: Local variation on a global theme?" *Public Administration* 83, 3: 709–733.

Van Helden, J., and Reichard, C. 2016. "Commonalities and differences in public and private sector performance management practices: a literature review." In *Performance Measurement and Management Control: Contemporary Issues*, edited by Epstein, M., Verbeeten, F., and Widener, S., 309–351. Emerald.

Van Helden, J.G., Johnsen, Å., and Vakkuri, J. 2008. "Distinctive research patterns on public sector performance measurement of public administration and accounting disciplines." *Public Management Review* 10, 5: 641–651.

Hood, C. 1991. "A public management for all seasons?." *Public Administration* 69, 1: 3–19.

Hood, C. 1995. "The 'new public management' in the 1980s: Variations on a theme." *Accounting, Organizations and Society* 20, 2–3: 93–109.

Hood, C., and Peters, G. 2004. "The middle aging of new public management: into the age of paradox?." *Journal of Public Administration Research and Theory* 14, 3: 267–282.

Hoskin, K. 2015. "What about the box? Some thoughts on the possibility of 'corruption prevention', and of 'the disciplined and ethical subject'." *Critical Perspectives on Accounting* 28: 71–81.

Hoskin, K.W., and Macve, R.H. 1986. "Accounting and the examination: A genealogy of disciplinary power." *Accounting, Organizations & Society* 11, 2: 105–136.

Hyndman, N., and Lapsley, I. 2016. "New public management: The story continues." *Financial Accountability & Management* 32, 4: 385–408.

Hyndman, N., Liguori, M., Meyer, R.E., Polzer, T., Rota, S., and Seiwald, J. 2014. "The translation and sedimentation of accounting reforms. A comparison of the UK, Austrian and Italian experiences." *Critical Perspectives on Accounting* 25, 4–5: 388–408.

Kartalis, N., Tsamenyi, M., and Jayasinghe, K. 2016. "Accounting in new public management (NPM) and shifting organizational boundaries: Evidence from the Greek Show Caves." *Accounting, Auditing & Accountability Journal* 29, 2: 248–277.

Kettl, D.F., and Kelman, S. 2007. *Reflections on 21st Century Government Management*. IBM Center for the Business of Government.

Key, V.O. 1940. "The lack of a budgetary theory." *American Political Science Review* 34, 6: 1137–1144.

Kroll, A. 2015. "Drivers of performance information use: Systematic literature review and directions for future research." *Public Performance & Management Review* 38, 3: 459–486.

Kurunmaki, L., Lapsley, I., and Melia, K. 2003. "Accountingization v. legitimation: A comparative study of the use of accounting information in intensive care." *Management Accounting Research* 14, 2: 112–139.

Lapsley, I. 2009. "New public management: The cruellest invention of the human spirit?" *Abacus* 45, 1: 1–21.

Liguori, M. 2012. "Radical change, accounting and public sector reforms: A comparison of Italian and Canadian municipalities." *Financial Accountability & Management* 28, 4: 437–463.

Liguori, M., Sicilia, M., and Steccolini, I. 2012. "Some like it non-financial... Politicians' and managers' views on the importance of performance information." *Public Management Review* 14, 7: 903–922.

Lorenz, C. 2012. "If you're so smart, why are you under surveillance? Universities, neoliberalism, and new public management." *Critical Inquiry* 38, 3: 599–629.

Lynn, Jr, L.E. 1998. "The new public management: How to transform a theme into a legacy." *Public Administration Review* 58, 3: 231–237.

Mauro, S.G., Cinquini, L., and Pianezzi, D. 2019. "New Public Management between reality and illusion: Analysing the validity of performance-based budgeting." *The British Accounting Review*. https://doi.org/10.1016/j.bar.2019.02.007.

Modell, S. 2004. "Performance measurement myths in the public sector: A research note." *Financial Accountability & Management* 20,1: 39–55.

Morales, J., Gendron, Y., and Guénin-Paracini, H. 2014. "State privatization and the unrelenting expansion of neoliberalism: The case of the Greek financial crisis." *Critical Perspectives on Accounting* 25, 6: 423–445.

Moynihan, D.P. 2015. "Uncovering the circumstances of performance information use findings from an experiment." *Public Performance & Management Review* 39, 1: 33–57.

Moynihan, D.P., and Pandey, S.K. 2010. "The big question for performance management: Why do managers use performance information?." *Journal of Public Administration Research & Theory* 20, 4: 849–866.

Mussari, R. 2017. "Public budgeting from a managerial perspective." In *The Routledge Handbook of Global Public Policy and Administration*, edited by Klassen, D.C. and Thomas R., 360–372. Routledge.

O'Flynn, J. 2007. "From new public management to public value: Paradigmatic change and managerial implications." *Australian Journal of Public Administration* 66, 3: 353–366.

Olson, O., Guthrie, J., and Humphrey, C. 1998. *Global Warning! Debating International Developments in New Public Financial Management*. Cappelen Akademisk Forlag.

Osborne, D., and Gaebler T. 1992. *Reinventing Government: How the Entrepreneurial Spirit is Transforming the Public Sector*. Addison-Wesley Publishing Co.

Pollitt, C., and Bouckaert, G. 2004. *Public Management Reform: A Comparative Analysis*. Oxford University Press.

Pollitt, C., and Bouckaert, G. 2011. *Public Management Reform: A Comparative Analysis of NPM, the Neo-Weberian State, and New Public Governance*. Oxford University Press.

Power, M. 1997. *The Audit Society: Rituals of Verification*. Oxford University Press.

Power, M., and Laughlin, R. 1992. "Critical theory and accounting." In *Critical Management Studies*, edited by Alvesson, M. and Willmott, H., 113–135. Sage.

Rubin, I.S., 2010. *The Politics of Public Budgeting*. CQ Press.

Saliterer, I., and Korac, S. 2013. "Performance information use by politicians and public managers for internal control and external accountability purposes." *Critical Perspectives on Accounting* 24, 7–8: 502–517.

Saliterer, I., Sicilia M., and Steccolini I.. 2017. "Public budgets and budgeting: State of the art and future challenges." In *Handbook of Public Administration and Management in Europe*, edited by E. Ongaro and S. Van Thiel, 141–163. Palgrave.

Sarker, E.A. 2006. "New public management in developing countries: An analysis of success and failure with particular reference to Singapore and Bangladesh." *International Journal of Public Sector Management* 19, 2: 180–203.

Schick, A. 1966. "The road to PPB: The stages of budget reform." *Public Administration Review* 26, 4: 243–258.

Skelley, B.D. 2002. "The ambiguity of results: Assessments of the new public management." *Public Administration and Management* 7, 2: 168–187.

Steccolini, I. 2019. "Accounting and the post-new public management. *Accounting, Auditing & Accountability Journal* 32, 1: 255–279.

Sterck, M. 2007. "The impact of performance budgeting on the role of the legislature: A four-country study." *International Review of Administrative Sciences* 73, 2: 189–203.

Stiglitz, J.E. 1989. *The Economic Role of the State*. Blackwell.

Talbot, C. 2005. "Performance management." In *The Oxford Handbook of Public Management*, edited by Ferlie, E., Laurence, E., Lynn, Jr., and Pollitt, C. Oxford University Press.

Talbot, C. 2010. *Theories of performance: Organizational and service improvement in the public domain*. Oxford University Press.

Tambulasi, R.I. 2009. "All that glisters is not gold: New public management and corruption in Malawi's local governance." *Development Southern Africa* 26, 2: 173–188.

Taylor, J. 2009. "Strengthening the link between performance measurement and decision making." *Public Administration* 87, 4: 853–871.

Van Thiel, S., and Leeuw, F.L. 2002. "The performance paradox in the public sector." *Public Performance & Management Review* 25, 3: 267–281.

Vakkuri, J. 2010. "Struggling with ambiguity: Public managers as users of NPM-oriented management instruments." *Public Administration* 88,4: 999–1024.

De Vries, M., and Nemec, J. 2013. "Public sector reform: An overview of recent literature and research on NPM and alternative paths." *International Journal of Public Sector Management* 26, 1: 4–16.

De Vries, M.S., Nemec, J., and Špaček, D. 2019. *Performance-Based Budgeting in the Public Sector*. Palgrave Macmillan.

Van de Walle, S., and Groeneveld, S. 2016. *Theory and Practice of Public Sector Reform*. Routledge.

Wildavsky, A.B. 1964. *Politics of the Budgetary Process*. Boston: Little, Brown & Co.

2 Empirical evidence on reforms in the NPM era

2.1 Performance: Empirical insights into conceptualization and measurement

Measuring and managing performance have been claimed as priorities in the agendas of public sector organizations worldwide and have significantly influenced different public services, including the higher education field. Over the last few decades, universities have increasingly adopted performance measurement and management systems consistent with the managerial process of reforms taking place in the higher education field. Specifically, the identity of universities has been reshaped by growing internationalization and marketization, which have put higher competitive pressures on universities (Ferlie et al. 2008; Parker 2002). These institutions are required to account for the results achieved and demonstrate their 'quality' to build their image across national borders and obtain a good positioning in educational rankings (Dixon et al. 2013; Espeland and Sauder 2016). This trend has been corroborated by the decrease in funds available, which increases competition among universities and stimulates the implementation of mechanisms designed to build government funding on performance assessment (Guthrie and Neumann 2007). This explains why universities have developed their performance measurement systems to measure and communicate their performance in an attempt to be viewed as attractive and secure additional resources. Journal and educational rankings, citation indices, and student satisfaction surveys are examples of performance tools used by universities to monitor results, and their development has been reinforced by the recent spread of digitalization as the increased use of the new language of H-index to express excellence demonstrates (van Houtum and van Uden 2020; Nørreklit et al. 2019).

Despite the numerous expectations attached to performance measurement and management systems, as anticipated in the previous chapter, several problematic issues can be identified (Andersen et al. 2016; Talbot 2010):

1. Unit of analysis:
   a. What entity is being measured? How are its boundaries set? At what level should performance be measured (e.g. university-level, department-level, or individual-level)?
2. Identity of stakeholders:
   a. Who are the actors involved? Who decides what a good performance is, and for whom?
3. Conceptual problems:
   a. What does performance mean? What should be included in its assessment? What should be excluded?
4. Technical problems:
   a. What indicators and measures are to be developed? Are these measures subjective? Are they formally and explicitly defined?
5. Value issues:
   a. To what values does performance measurement respond?

These issues can be observed in the higher education field, which provides an exemplary context of observation about how numbers guide, govern, and influence who we are and what we do (Kurunmäki et al. 2016).

First, complexity emerges from the multiple levels at which performance should be measured. Indeed, performance can be measured at the individual level through performance assessments of professors and researchers; these evaluations are then used to manage their careers. Performance can also be measured at the department level to make allocative decisions, and finally at the university level to guarantee a strong comprehensive performance and positioning in the rankings.

Second, who decides when a university is performing well and towards whom (e.g. to students or society)? This is another important challenge strongly related to the conceptual problems that clearly emerge in defining the meaning of performance. When does a university perform well? Taking into account that a university can fulfil different functions, such as teaching, researching, and producing knowledge for the community, what should be included in the performance measurement and management system? Further, how should different aspects be integrated and balanced? Consequently, it becomes difficult to operationalize such measurement.

Indicators, measures, and targets are difficult to design, and the risk is that there is a tendency towards measuring inputs and outputs instead of outcomes through the adoption of quantitative rather than qualitative approaches (Grossi et al. 2020). For instance, measures of outputs can be represented by the number of articles published in academic journals, the number of research projects won, and the number of graduate students enrolled. On the other hand, measuring community service and third-role activities is rarer (Alach 2017), and measuring the quality and impact is even more complex and challenging (Kallio et al. 2017). A critique has been that quantitative performance measures tend to ignore quality issues because they are more difficult to measure, and consequently quality becomes a number and quantity and control replace freedom, novelty, and societal benefits (e.g. Verbeeten 2008; van Houtum and van Uden 2020). This may produce problematic consequences. For instance, the prevalent use of a quantitative orientation has worsened the motivation of academic actors to engage in creative and knowledge-intensive work and has increased stagnation and conformity (Gendron 2008; Kallio and Kallio 2014). In such contexts, the academic actor becomes an academic performer (Gendron 2008) concerned about his or her performance rather than about the value to create. The pervasive use of metrics has reshaped academic values, identities, and roles (Agyemang and Broadbent 2015). This recalls the last criticality previously listed, pointing to the effects of the evaluative and managerial culture on traditional academic values (Espeland and Sauder 2016; van Helden and Argento 2020; Pianezzi et al. 2019). Under the managerialism pressures, academics themselves may contribute to marginalize academic demands in university governance through the use of accounting (Aleksandrov 2020).

The integrated and comprehensive consideration of these problematic issues may explain why performance measurement systems may appear to be adopted only in a symbolic manner (Dobija et al. 2019) and considered unsuitable for assessing scientific quality (Kallio et al. 2017). This suggests the need to develop an outcome-based approach suitable for shifting the attention towards the outcome to realize and the value to produce with a long-term perspective. Further, this emphasizes the need of improving performance measures and information in order to reinforce their effective use in the decision-making process. The growing relevance of accounting requires proper development and use of accounting tools and information.

2.2 Budgeting: Empirical insights into performance-based budgeting

2.2.1 An introduction to performance-based budgeting: Dead or alive?

In the NPM-era, budget reforms are often at the heart of the academic debate because of the widespread recognition of the need for a shift from a traditional incremental to a rational approach to budgeting. The rational approach is built on performance. Performance-based budgeting (PBB) is not a new practice and its history can be traced back to state and local reforms advocated in the USA since the early part of the twentieth century and expanded in the 1950s (Ho et al. 2019). This was followed through with several efforts related to programme budgeting and the planning-programming-budgeting system (Kong 2005; Moynihan and Beazley 2016). Hence, PBB is a well-known concept in public financial management and has metamorphosed numerous times over several decades (Schick 2014). In the era of NPM, it gained new emphasis and became increasingly attractive for various governments worldwide (Anessi-Pessina et al. 2016; Hijal-Moghrabi 2017). Within the NPM-oriented process of reforms aimed at rationalizing decision-making and strengthening efficiency and effectiveness, PBB has gained relevance since it was considered a useful tool for achieving a 'performing state' through a performing budget (Shick 2003). In an era of growing concerns about public expenditures, higher expectations, and significant constraints, PBB can be seen as a tool for strategic steering and control (Mussari et al. 2016).

The key element that distinguishes PBB from other budgeting approaches and processes is the focus on results (see Box 2.1 for a brief overview of budgeting processes). Performance measures and information are expected to be produced and used to support budgetary decision-making by politicians, managers, and public servants; the actors involved are made accountable for the results. The integration of performance information is expected to take place throughout the budgeting process, from preparation to execution and auditing. This focus on results and the rational expectation that performance information can be directly integrated into decision-making explain why PBB has gained renewed interest in the spirit of NPM (Gruening 2001). According to this latter paradigm, performance undoubtedly plays a key role in management and budgeting activities. Thus, PBB – as an example of a results-oriented reform – and NPM can be considered interdependent but distinct innovations (Schick 2014).

**BOX 2.1: AN OVERVIEW OF
BUDGETING PROCESSES**

Over time, the approaches to budgeting have been various. One of the most traditional budgeting processes is represented by the so-called 'incremental budgeting', whereby the budget for the upcoming year is formulated by updating the current budget for expected changes (e.g. price inflation for goods used by the organization). Incrementalism has been a pre-eminent theory of budgeting, being supported by an age of economic growth and government expansion until the late 1970s (Wildavsky 1964; Schick 1983).

Although incremental budgeting can be considered a simple and easy process, it is not able to respond to significant changes in the environment and it does not motivate a re-thinking and scrutiny of the budget, which remains pretty stable over time.

To overcome the main limitations of incremental budgeting, other approaches have been developed, such as the planning-programming-budgeting system, known under the acronym PPBS. This is a different approach to budgeting, built on the careful identification of programmes, programme objectives, costs of programmes, and detailed analyses of alternatives. It was introduced into the US Department of Defense in 1961 and then extended to the federal budget. According to PPBS, the alternatives to achieve the objectives of government programmes should be compared and assessed according to their costs and benefits in order to make the final choice (Kelly 2005). The period in which PPBS has been developed is a period regarded as the golden age of planning (Pollitt and Bouckaert 2011) and accordingly the budgeting process has been built on rational planning and has emphasized the relevance of programmes. PPBS represents an exemplary attempt at introducing rationality into budgetary decision-making (Mussari 2017). However, also this approach to budgeting has been contested in practice, paving the way to further budgeting reforms.

In this regard, the zero-based budgeting process can be mentioned. As the name suggests, according to this process, the budget is formulated by starting from 'zero' every year, requiring the organization to reflect and justify every item in the budget. On the one hand, this approach is suitable for focusing and constantly reflecting on priorities and policies. On the other hand, it is complex and time-consuming. As occurred with previous reforms, also in this case the critiques have stimulated further changes.

Among the other prominent budgeting approaches, it is worth mentioning performance-based budgeting, discussed in this chapter, which has been revitalized in the NPM era despite its origins being traced back to the 1950s, and the more recent reform of participatory budgeting, which is discussed in Chapter 4.

This constant process of change confirms that 'budgeting must be an adaptive process if it is to retain central importance for governments' (Schick 1983, 24).

Over time, PBB has been given several labels, such as performance budgeting, output/outcome budgeting, and results-oriented budgeting (Jordon and Hackbart 1999; Kong 2005; Thompson 1994). Although these various labels have been used interchangeably, they may also reflect a deeper variation in the interpretation of the practice. The diversity in the labels can be combined with a diversity of interpretations, as there is no standardized and widely accepted definition of PBB. In this regard, the first dimension that explains variation is represented by the type of performance information to be used in the budgeting process. For instance, while performance budgeting refers to *performance* in more general terms, both output and outcome-based budgeting are more specific and indicate the type of performance information that must be utilized to inform the budgeting process.

Another dimension that drives conceptual variation is concerned with how the integration of performance information in the budgeting process must take place. Indeed, the interpretation of PBB can range from the consideration that '*a performance budget is **any budget that represents information** on what agencies have done or expect to do with the money provided to them*' (Schick 2003, 101, emphasis added), to a more focused definition according to which performance budgeting is '*a form of budgeting that relates funds allocated to measurable results*' (OECD 2007, 20, emphasis added) or '*a budget that explicitly links each increment in resources to an increment in outputs or other results*' (Schick 2003, 101). The relationship between funds and results has been explicitly recalled and emphasized in other definitions, as evident in the following definition of performance budgets elaborated by Robinson and Brumby (2005):

> '*[P]rocedures or mechanisms intended to **strengthen links** between the funds provided to public sector entities and their **outcomes and/or outputs** through the **use of formal performance information in resource allocation** decision-making*'.
>
> (Robinson and Brumby, 2005, 5, emphasis added.)

To reflect and recognize the multiple potential uses of performance information in the budgeting process, even in light of the long history of PBB, its challenging implementation, and the criticalities faced by governments worldwide, the OECD has elaborated the following working definition according to which PBB is:

> '*[T]he use of performance information to inform budget decisions, whether as a direct input to budget allocation decisions or as contextual information and/or inputs to budget planning, as well as to instil greater*

transparency and accountability throughout the budget process, by providing information to the public on performance objectives and results'.
(OECD 2019, 116.)

As this definition suggests, different categories of PBB can be identified according to the way in which performance information is integrated in the budgeting process and according to the purpose PBB is expected to achieve; each category is assigned a different label (see Box 2.2).

BOX 2.2: A CATEGORIZATION OF PBB

Countries have experimented with the introduction of performance elements in the budgeting process and different models of PBB have been identified over time. According to the OECD (2007), it was initially possible to identify the following three categories:

- **Presentational performance budgeting**: Performance information is reported but not explicitly used to inform the budgeting process. This approach is relatively easy to implement and is appropriate when the objective is limited to showing that allocations are responsive to government objectives and priorities.
- **Performance-informed budgeting**: Performance information is produced and included in budget documents and utilized to re-prioritize the expenditures on the basis of performance. Performance information is used to inform budget decisions along with other information, but there is no automatic or mechanical linkage between targets or performance results and funding.
- **Direct/formula performance budgeting**: Establishes a direct link between results and resources, thereby implying a budgetary response to over- or under-achievement of performance objectives.

This categorization has been enriched over time due to the experiences of different countries with PBB and the challenges faced in using performance information. A fourth category was added by the OECD (2019):

- **Managerial performance budgeting**: A variant of performance-informed budgeting, with a focus on managerial impacts and changes in organizational behaviour.

The OECD classification focuses on the type of utilization of performance information in the budgeting process, although it is not always easy to assess the use of performance information and to clearly design the boundaries, for instance, between presentational budgeting and performance-informed budgeting.

In addition to the extent to which performance information is incorporated in the budget, considering the span of performance (cf. Bouckaert and Halligan 2008) and the nature and embeddedness of the link between financial and non-financial performance information, other variables include the type of performance objective and indicators (outcome, output, process, input) and the availability of both past and future performance information. In this regard, a recent empirical study (Bleyen et al. 2017) proposes the following categorization of PBB:

- **Embryonic performance budgeting**: A preliminary and unclear link exists between financial and non-financial information, without any budget coverage.
- **Target performance budgeting**: The link between financial and non-financial performance information is much more developed and all parts of the budget are covered with future performance objectives.
- **Performance budgeting for results**: Both qualitative and quantitative data and both future and past performance information are incorporated in the budget.

Therefore, the use of different terms by governments may be considered useful for distinguishing practices according to their level of sophistication, thereby representing a semantic splitting aligned with practice development (Joyce 2011). The different categories of PBB, as previously discussed, can be considered as a continuum (Schick 2014) according to which governments can implement PBB following an incremental path.

This perspective reveals the importance of a flexible approach to PBB, recognizing that the practice can be used for different purposes and may require to be revised and adapted according to the needs and peculiarities of the setting (ter Bogt et al. 2015; Mauro et al. 2017; Nielsen and Baekgaard 2015). In this regard, it is widely accepted that PBB cannot be considered a universal concept, as it is affected by several variables. Accordingly, its design can and must change across and within the same country, as there is no 'one-size-fits-all' approach (e.g. Helmuth 2010). Therefore, the proliferation of labels, conceptualizations, and categorizations of PBB is reflected in the variety of adoption and implementation approaches. For example, PBB can be introduced through legislation, in a top–down and centralized or bottom–up and decentralized manner, in a comprehensive manner (e.g. by involving all the ministries) or through partial coverage, or in a big bang or incremental step-by-step reform process (OECD 2007).

The academic debate on the practice indicates that PBB has a long history characterized by both successes and, often, limited results and has undergone peaks and troughs, thereby undermining its credibility (Ho 2011; Hou et al. 2011; Pitsvada and Lo Stracco 2002; Schick 2003). Previous studies have indicated that the success or failure of PBB may be determined by the existence of a 'reform space' within which the reform can be adopted and implemented (Andrews 2004). This reform space is determined by the presence of several key factors, which can be summarized in the following manner: Authority, ability, and acceptance (Andrews 2004). In order to be successfully implemented, PBB, just like any other public sector reform, requires the support of politicians and managers. In particular, previous studies have claimed that the existence of legislation on PBB can support the implementation of this reform (Lu et al. 2009). Further, PBB builds on the need of elaborating insightful performance measures to be appropriately interpreted and used. Therefore, the appropriateness of data produced and the type of information elaborated contribute to the success of PBB, together with organizational, contextual, and individual factors (Grossi et al. 2016). Hence, staff competency, information technology systems, task complexity, and the inherent ambiguity of performance information are all variables that have a crucial influence on PBB (ter Bogt et al. 2015; Moynihan 2005). An exemplary source of ambiguity that influences PBB concerns the interpretation of performance results: If a programme or a department performs poorly, does it mean that it should be terminated or it requires additional resources (Caiden 1998)? Providing an answer to this question may be considered a political discourse. Public budget remains a political process built on negotiations among multiple actors. The commitment towards the reform, its acceptance by the different actors, and the balance of interests are crucial factors for the success of PBB. Accordingly, considering the nature of public budgeting, it could be said that the functioning of PBB may depend on the behaviour and skills of politicians and also civil servants, and crucial obstacles are represented by rigid budgets, political pressures, and the risk of persistent incremental norms (Schick 2014).

Consistent with the complexity of the reform, the academic debate on the topic has revealed that the use of performance information in the context of budgeting has been relevant but highly challenging and remains rather limited overall (e.g. Grossi et al. 2016; Mauro et al. 2018).

In particular, the criticalities linked to the possible uses of performance information in the budgeting process have sparked a debate on what *should* be the better use of PBB. Many have questioned whether PBB is a management or budgeting tool (e.g. Ho 2011; Hou et al. 2011). The approach to PBB has indeed also been wide, as revealed by the following conceptualization of the practice:

> '[P]erformance-based budgeting is actually **a more diverse set of requirements**, blending various aspects of current public management trends, including outcome measurement, performance measurement systems, strategic planning and benchmarking'.
> (Melkers and Willoughby 2001, 55, emphasis added.)

This approach reveals the embeddedness of PBB into a wider context of managerial reforms. In addition to the 'core' forms of PBB, which are built on the use of performance information, the label has been flexibly used to include 'PBB extenders', as programme evaluation, spending reviews (Schick 2014), which can be considered as tools that support PBB rather than examples of PBB. This indicates that the conceptual views on the role of PBB have been varying. This reflects, on the one hand, the interpretation of PBB as a transformation of the budget which requires a change in how budgetary appropriations are made and, on the other hand, the consideration of PBB as an enrichment/value-added resource for budget-makers (Schick 2014).

Previous studies have empirically analyzed and showed that the initiative of PBB was more popular as a management and accountability tool than as an allocative tool (e.g. Jordan and Hackbart 2005; Melkers and Willoughby 2001; Wang 2000). According to the perceptions of users, particularly budgeters, PBB appears to have a greater effect on organizational and programme-related factors, such as programme accountability and effectiveness as well as general decision-making (Jordan and Hackbart 2005; Melkers and Willoughby 2001). Recent surveys conducted across OECD countries confirm that PBB has been more successful as a communication tool to increase transparency rather than as a resource allocation tool (OECD 2019). However, previous studies have supported the theory that PBB can be viewed as an integral part of management and budgeting reform (Ho 2011). Governments cannot budget for results if they do not manage for results. It has been theorized that it can be useful for practitioners and the academic community to discuss **performance-based budget management (PBM)** (Ho 2018). This perspective focuses more on the financial management aspects of the practice, where PBM is expected to integrate several activities that range from multi-year budgetary planning to policy planning to micro budget planning at the programme and departmental levels. PBB cannot imply a dichotomy between an allocative tool or a management tool due to the constant tension existing between allocation and management. It must be adopted and adapted to the setting. Accordingly, numerous different theoretical perspectives have been identified to explain the success or failure of PBB (Ho et al. 2019; Ho 2018), thereby interpreting its potential different role. These perspectives range from interpreting PBB as an organizational change process, requiring changes in numerous managerial systems, to PBB as a political process, a communicative process used to support information exchange, or as a principal–agent challenge implying negotiations among multiple actors. However, these theoretical perspectives can be considered interrelated since there are overlapping elements and issues that can be simultaneously found in practice.

Currently, the practice remains a subject of debate regarding whether the current trend towards PBB is well designed and how it can perform in the future. Over a decade ago, Pitsvada and Lo Stracco (2002) published a work entitled 'Performance budgeting – the next budgetary answer. But what is the question?'. Is PBB useful for public sector organizations to cope with the current problems? Or is it only 'old wine in a new bottle?' (Martin 1997). Is it destined to fail again as in the past while traditional budget will last (Wildavsky 1978)? These questions are still actual.

Despite the challenges and criticalities linked to the implementation and use of PBB, it continues to be investigated by researchers (e.g. Mauro et al. 2017; Lu et al. 2015) and to be on the agenda of numerous public sector organizations worldwide. According to the results of the most recent OECD survey, the adoption of PBB is widespread but limited. It is limited since the majority of OECD countries apply a centralized or standardized PB framework for the central government; however, financial data continues to have a predominant role in budget negotiations with the central budget authority (Martì 2019). The adoption is widespread since PBB is implemented not only in Anglo-Saxon countries – where the orientation towards performance measurement and management has been historically predominant – but also in other developed countries and in several countries in transitional and developmental conditions (De Vries et al. 2019; Ho et al. 2019). The still active interest in the practice is testified by the efforts put in developing PBB by international organizations like the OECD. The OECD Network of Senior Budget Officials (SBOs) has shown a constant interest in the relationship between budgetary governance and performance management initiatives. In 2004, the SBOs established a performance and results network to increase the understanding of these practices. In addition, several OECD surveys on the development of PBB in member countries have been conducted (2007, 2011, 2016, and 2018). In 2019, a report on good practices for performance budgeting was published based on these surveys, on the OECD country budget reviews, and on recent studies published by the OECD, the World Bank, and the International Monetary Fund. In 2015, the European Commission also showed an interest in PBB by initiating the project called Budget Focused on Results. The following box introduces this recent initiative (see Box 2.3), which can be considered an example of the continuous interest in PBB in the public sector.

BOX 2.3: PERFORMANCE BUDGETING AND THE EUROPEAN COMMISSION

The website of the European Commission states, '*The EU Budget Focused on Results (BFOR) initiative was started in 2015 to join efforts of EU institutions, governments and civil society towards better spending, increased accountability and transparency, and creating a maximum added value for EU citizens*'.

The BFOR is an initiative launched by the European Commission to emphasize the role of performance in the budgeting process. It represents an additional step forward in the process of reforming the Commission, which had already established a budget performance framework that relied on the strategic planning and programming (SPP) cycle. Performance information is an element of the EU budgetary system, as indicators, targets, and evaluations are produced.

The BFOR project was specifically designed to guarantee that resources are allocated to priorities, financed projects perform well, and a coherent balance between compliance and performance is achieved. In order to fulfil these aims, the conceptual framework of the project is built on four pillars:

1. Where does the money go?
2. How do we spend it?
3. How do we assess the performance of the EU budget?
4. How do we communicate?

The rationale underlying this cycle is to begin with the identification of programmes that add value and contribute to implementing the overall strategy and priorities (pillar 1), and then to proceed with the measurement and achievement of efficiency and simplicity in the procedures (pillar 2). Finally, a robust performance framework must enable the assessment of the results achieved with EU funds (pillar 3) and lead to appropriate and transparent communication (pillar 4).

This project exemplifies an approach to performance budgeting informed by the systematic use of performance information in order to improve transparency, accountability, and the use of the resources.

Source: https://ec.europa.eu/info/strategy/eu-budget/
achievements/budget-results_en

In light of this discussion, it can be said that PBB remains alive, although it calls for a re-conceptualization. A strict and rigid rationalist interpretation of PBB may result in unsatisfactory results, as evident from empirical experiences with PBB (e.g. the limited use of performance information in budgetary negotiations). The following sub-sections provide empirical insights into experiences with PBB across countries, emphasizing the need for rethinking it without completely abandoning it.

2.2.2 An insight into experiences in southern Europe: The case of Italy

Traditionally, central government budgeting, accounting, and reporting systems in Italy have been cash and commitment based. The main purpose of this approach was to guarantee budgetary compliance and expenditure control (Liguori et al. 2018). These systems have been subject to a long experimentation and reform process, since Italy has introduced several modifications to public sector financial management and budgeting process over the last several decades and further changes continue to be made to the budget process in order to address important weaknesses as they are identified (Blöndal et al. 2016). In particular, since the 1990s, performance information and data have assumed increasing recognition, and line ministries were required to identify target objectives, resource requirements, and performance indicators in the so-called 'preliminary notes', which were notes preliminary to the budget. The influence of NPM has played a predominant role in guiding these institutional reforms and addressing the lack of specific attention paid to cost control, efficiency, and effectiveness (Borgonovi 1996).

In order to overcome the limits of the budget – still overly complex, with numerous expenditure items, a persistent incremental logic, and an emphasis on controls (Liguori et al. 2018) – the structure of the budget underwent transformation. The budget was organized into missions and each mission included several programmes. A mission indicates the overall purpose for which resources are being spent, and programmes are homogenous groups of activities by which a mission can be achieved. The new structure of the budget was designed to improve the linkage between resources and results to achieve the strengthening of both allocative and operative efficiency, thereby improving transparency and accountability (Servizio del Bilancio del Senato 2007).

In addition to the reform of the budget structure, performance management systems have been reformed in 2009, mandating the introduction of a formal performance management system within the central government. An integrated and comprehensive performance system called the 'performance cycle' was adopted to control and improve the overall governmental performance (Cepiku et al. 2017). It is necessary for the cycle to define objectives that must be attained and set targets and indicators for each objective, link objectives to resource allocation, monitor the execution of the objectives during the year to adopt the necessary corrective actions, measure and assess individual and organizational performance, use awards to valorize merit, and report results to all internal and external stakeholders. This performance cycle must be developed in accordance with the budgetary planning cycle, with objectives linked to the allocation of resources following the enactment of budget legislation.

Further, two key documents were mandated by the new legislation: The 'performance plan' and the 'performance report'. The performance plan is a three-year planning document elaborated and published by each ministry at the beginning of each year. The plan is adopted based on the policy directions for each ministry and accordingly it defines strategic and operational objectives, which are set according to the policies defined by the minister. The plan identifies the targets and performance indicators for each objective. The performance report is an annual document elaborated at the end of the year and published by June of the year following the reference year. It closes the performance cycle as a reporting document, whereby each ministry accounts for the results it achieved as compared to those initially established in the performance plan.

These documents must be aligned with the budgeting documents. The integrative notes to the budget, which are derived from further development of the previous preliminary notes, are prepared by each ministry and are attached to the national budget estimates. The notes were initially required to indicate the objectives that must be achieved for each programme, the indicators and targets that must be used to monitor their enactment, the resources allocated, and the budgeted costs. The performance information reported in the notes must be coherent with that reported in the performance plans. A selection of indicators and targets included in the performance plans must be included in the notes. At the end of the year, in the integrative notes to the final statement, the respective results are reported in terms of results achieved, resources used, and costs incurred. Thus, the cycle is closed coherently at the end of each reference period through performance reports.

These reforms set the ground for PBB. In 2009, the Ministry of Economy and Finance (MEF) published an official report entitled 'Performance-budgeting, public spending and institutional context: The Italian experience'. This document emphasized the need to revise the process and mechanisms of public spending in Italy and reinforce performance measurement practices following the examples of other European countries. In this document, PBB was defined as a budgeting procedure, whereby the allocation of public resources is conditioned by the results achieved towards policy goals in relation to the resources employed. Each programme is assigned to a specific department which is responsible for its realization. Information on results is expected to influence allocation decisions and this must be realized through the coordination between two cycles: the performance cycle (performance plan and report) and the budgeting cycle (integrative notes to the budget and to the final statement). The effort at integrating these different cycles is an attempt to transform the legal framework by employing an organizational and managerial approach (Bianchi and Xavier 2017) and results from the attempts to integrate the financial, strategic, and operating planning systems (Ranalli and Giosi 2011).

This reform has been comprehensive in scope, introducing homogeneous requirements for all central organizations (ministries) of the Italian state. The legislation assigned each organization the possibility of adopting a system for measuring and managing performance, whereby each organization could specify phases, execution times, actors, and responsibilities of the system within the broader legal framework. The centralized adoption of the reform was balanced with a partial flexibility to ministers. However, in practice, the systems established by ministries were highly similar despite their different organizational contexts (Mauro et al. 2018).

The reforms have been managed in a centralized fashion, and a national authority was required to support the performance cycle and develop guidelines for all departments of the central government. New guidelines released in 2017 for the elaboration of the performance plans by the Department of Public Function and its technical commission partially replaced the previous guidelines, thereby attempting to address the main problems emerging from previous experimentation through an interactive approach that involves active collaboration with each ministry, as the decision to start in advance the planning phase of the plan of performance.

Recent reforms have further revised the budget structure and the link between the performance cycle and budgeting process. Since 2017 the budget has been organized into missions, programmes, and actions: Actions have been added in order to make the final purpose of spending more evident. The reform requires that objectives are linked to each programme and elaborated with reference to the programme actions. An objective can be linked to more than one action, while an action can be linked only to one objective. According to the last reform, it is no longer required to link resources to objectives. Nevertheless, the relevance of the integration between the performance cycle and the budgeting process is still recognized (see Box 2.4).

BOX 2.4: PBB IN ITALY

According to the reforms of the budget and performance management system, the ministries in Italy are required to produce and publish, among other documents, the integrative notes to the budget and to the financial statement (budgeting cycle) and the performance plans and reports (performance cycle), which are interlinked.

In the performance plan, it is possible to identify the resources allocated to each mission and programme, and in more detail, to each action. The actions are identified within a mission and a programme, as shown by the following table (Table 2.1).

Table 2.1 A top-down approach

Mission: ...			
Programme: ...			
	Year 1	Year 2	Year 3
Action 1: ...	*Resources allocated*	*Resources allocated*	*Resources allocated*
Action 2: ...	*Resources allocated*	*Resources allocated*	*Resources allocated*
Action *n*: ...	*Resources allocated*	*Resources allocated*	*Resources allocated*

In addition to the indication of the resources, the performance plan reports the objectives linked to programme and actions. The plan then details the indicators linked to each objective, specifying the type of indicators, and indicating the target to be achieved, how it is measured, and which data sources are used for this purpose. This allows the measurement of performance and the monitoring of objectives' achievement. The performance plan is coordinated with the integrative note to the budget.

The integrative note to the budget shows the resources allocated to each mission, programme, and action. In addition to the objectives, the note reports the indicators to be used to monitor the achievement of the objectives. The indicators can be indicators of financial realization which indicates the extent to which financial resources are consumed, indicators of physical realization which indicates the quantity of products and services delivered, output indicators which focus on the results of a programme, and outcome indicators which measure the impact on society (Angei and Tucci 2020). According to the report elaborated by the Ministry of Finance, 48,14% of the indicators reported in the integrative notes are output indicators, 33,97% are indicators of physical realization, 10,65% of indicators are of financial realization, and 7,24% are outcome indicators (Ministry of Finance, http://www.rgs.mef.gov.it/_Documenti/VERSIONE-I/Attivit--i/ Rendiconto/Note_integrative_a_consuntivo/2019/Relazione_al_rendiconto_2019.pdf). The performance indicators have been developed with the support of the Public Function Department in recent years with the aim of enhancing the development of a performance culture and benchmarking.

The logical structure beyond this document can be depicted as follows (Figure 2.1):

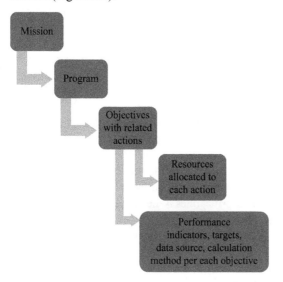

Figure 2.1 From the mission to the targets.

Therefore, in the integrative notes to the budget it is possible to find the resources allocated to each action, the objective linked to each action, and the indicators linked to each objective. This budgeting document hence reports non-financial information (including financial information).

At the end of the period, in the performance report, information on the results achieved is presented for each objective compared to what

> was stated in the performance plan, and in the integrative notes to the final statement there is an indication of resources used, costs incurred, and objectives achieved compared to what was stated in the integrative notes to the budget.

The stressful financial conditions and continuous political changes the government has faced (Rebora et al. 2017) have challenged the development of coherent and consistent policies. This has influenced the development of objectives and the related measurement and management of performance. Further, the comprehensive textbook approach adopted by the legislator to introduce PBB has not facilitated the implementation and utilization of the reform (Mauro et al. 2018), the results of which remain limited (Bonomi Savignon et al. 2019; Rebora et al. 2017). While it is possible to record an abundance of performance information, the use of information regarding results related to influencing decisions for the future has appeared partial, with a significant proportion of the indicators having an inherently bureaucratic nature. The duplication of documents and responsibilities has been recognized, thereby indicating the risk that the intended managerial reform could be transformed into an additional bureaucratic burden. According to the last OECD survey (2019), a performance budgeting framework exists and is compulsory at the central level of government in Italy; however, PBB still appears to be at the presentational level at the central level of government in Italy based on recent empirical evidence on PBB.

The emphasis placed on the performance and rationalization of the budget has resulted in an improvement in the performance measures produced but has not yet led to a relevant improvement in the utilization of performance information. One of the main criticalities is the limited use of the information on performance reported in the documents in order to support the planning activities for the next period. The integrative notes to the budget and to the financial statement (budgeting cycle) and the performance plan and report (performance cycle) pursue different purposes. The budgeting cycle documents are more oriented towards parliament, while the performance cycle documents are expected to orient the actions of the administrations and support the accountability towards citizens. Accordingly, it seems that the integration between the two cycles is interpreted as a form of coordination among documents and a coherence of their contents, but it is more difficult to integrate the use of performance information in the allocation process. The Italian mechanism to introduce managerial reforms through legislative decrees continues to appear as a paradox and does not support the spread of a managerial knowledge in the public sector: The 'management by decree' approach limits the development of managerial notions of accountability, performance, and control (Panozzo 2000). The theories leading decision-making should be adapted and properly translated in the context where they have to be adopted (Marcon 2011; Ongaro and Valotti 2008). The institutional context where the reforms are adopted and how they are adopted matter, especially when there is a high variation within the same country (Marcon and Panozzo 1998). In Italy, there are still cultural and technical obstacles to financial management reforms and the PBB reform appears partially implemented (Grossi et al. 2016; Mauro et al. 2018; Mussari et al. 2016).

2.2.3 An insight into Nordic countries: The cases of Finland and Sweden

Both Finland and Sweden have a long tradition with performance measurement and management systems; the countries adopted performance management and budgeting reforms in the early to mid-1990s (Curristine 2005). In this context, PBB was introduced as a component of management by objectives and this was in keeping with a shift to an NPM logic.

Specifically, in Sweden, in the late 1980s, budget reforms were intended to enable long-term planning, thereby abandoning incrementalism techniques and replacing rule-based input control systems with an emphasis on results and outcomes (Wilks 1995). A fixed medium-term framework through three-year expenditure ceilings was introduced along with a performance orientation (Downes et al. 2017). Non-financial performance targets were emphasized, and the budget was arranged around 27 'expenditure areas' as the structural basis for setting targets and reporting on results. In this context, the performance budgeting project, known by its Swedish acronym VESTA, was initiated in 1997 and added a non-financial information portion to the financial one in the budget (Gustaffson 2004; Sterck 2007). Several types of information are taken into account in the preparation of the budget. Before the government submits its budget proposal to parliament, many analyses must be produced as the basis for the government's decisions. This work is coordinated by the Ministry of Finance, but all ministries take part in providing background material (official website of the Government Offices of Sweden).

In Finland, PBB was also adopted in the context of performance-oriented reforms. The Ministry of Finance is responsible for developing financial steering systems for the central government in Finland. In 2005, it established a new conceptual scheme for providing performance measurement information: The so-called performance prism (see Box 2.5). In this context, in Finland, PBB was designed and introduced in order to strengthen *ex-ante* and *ex-post* accountability by supporting the budget proposal with performance targets and reporting the results in the final accounts. It was applied incrementally as 'a budgeting method in which the preparation of the budget proposal is governed and motivated by performance targets' (Salminen and Viitala 2006, 138) through a transition process since the end of the 1980s. Performance agreements between sector ministries and their agencies form the core of the system and they are morally, not legally, binding. In these multi-annual performance agreements between the ministry and each agency in its administrative branch, the available resources and the outcomes to be achieved through them are detailed, while the yearly appropriations are allocated to each central government agency in the state budget (official website of the Ministry of Finance). The targets and the needed resources to achieve them are negotiated between ministries and their agencies. The budget documentation contains targets for and reports on the outputs and outcomes. Indeed, the agencies report on the achievement of the agreed performance targets in the annual reports, and the ministries report on the performance of their sectors in the government annual report.

BOX 2.5: PERFORMANCE MANAGEMENT IN FINLAND

The inclusion of targets and performance information in the budget documentation, the introduction of accrual accounting, the extension of both audit function and managerial flexibility, and the elaboration of performance contracts were key elements of change in Finland (Blöndal et al. 2003). One of the most significant aspects is represented by the 'performance prism' created to describe the framework for setting targets and accountability, according to which a top–down approach is employed to define policies and measure them with a consequent bottom–up accountability (see the following representation; Salminen and Viitala 2006).

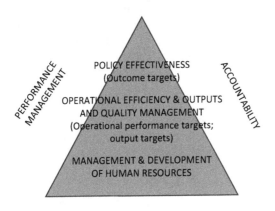

On the one hand, this prism allows for the identification of different types of targets designed to measure, respectively, policy effectiveness, operational efficiency, and quality management. The prism identifies the relationship among these targets: Outcome targets apply to broad benefits and impacts affecting society while output targets refer more directly to the operations of an agency. On the other hand, this prism is also suitable for explaining the accountability mechanisms. Indeed, how human resources are managed may influence the capacity of agencies to achieve operational targets, and consequently the operational results may influence the effectiveness of policies.

This prism is a fundamental piece of the performance management and budgeting system. Performance targets and information formulated in the different areas and at the different levels are then expected to be used to inform the budgetary negotiations and to justify the budget proposals and account for the results.

According to the last OECD survey, a performance budgeting framework is in place and is compulsory for line ministries and agencies in both Finland and Sweden; however, in Finland, PBB appears to be in the form of managerial performance budgeting and in Sweden it appears to be in the form of performance-informed budgeting (OECD, 2019). In particular, in Sweden, performance budgeting currently appears to be 'in a state of flux and internal review' (Downes et al. 2017, 12). In principle, the expenditure areas of the budget serve as the basis for setting high-level goals and indicators; however, in practice, the performance framework is not very systematic.

These results emphasize how performance budgeting may call for a rethinking even in the context of a stronger performance orientation and a long experience with performance measurement and management systems. Although governments may have rather developed performance systems, they can struggle with performance budgeting anyway (Mauro et al. 2019).

2.2.4 An insight into central-western European countries: The cases of Germany and the Netherlands

Since 2006, the Federal Ministry of Finance in Germany initiated a project to transform the system and modernize the budgeting and accounting systems; however, the reform was abandoned in 2010 (Jones and Lüder 2011). A significant portion of the reform was the inclusion of non-financial output measures for each product in the budget (Jones et al. 2013). Thus, a path towards PBB was undertaken. Moreover, a few changes towards PBB were also adopted at the state level, despite the limited results (Reichard and Küchler-Stahn 2019). According to the last OECD survey, a performance budgeting framework is in place and is compulsory for line ministries and agencies in Germany, although the adopted budgeting approach appears to be presentational (OECD 2019). According to this study, budget chapters include certain information to provide a policy context for allocations but do so without establishing clear linkages. However, recent studies clearly point out the persistence of a traditional approach to budgeting at the state and, especially, federal level (Reichard and Küchler-Stahn 2019), revealing the lack of a proper and well-developed orientation to performance budgeting.

Compared to the federal and state levels, a more significant reform path with reference to PBB has been undertaken at the local level. A relevant and comprehensive reform of financial management took place at the local government level in Germany at the beginning of 2000. Its implementation followed different paths across local governments, as some of them implemented the reform rather early after its introduction and others did it only later. Accrual accounting and accrual budgeting were adopted through the introduction of a set of core elements to be applied in each local government; however, given the German federalism, each local government was flexible in detailing the reform. Apart from the introduction of resource-based accounting and financial reporting, the new 'product budget' was a major highlight of the reform (Grossi et al. 2016). Indeed, this latter budgeting reform is particularly worthy of attention in this context because the budget has been designed as a performance budget. It is characterized by the following elements:

- A mid-term perspective is recommended
- Performance targets and indicators must be identified and measured
- Performance information must be elaborated and presented regarding the product groups or essential products in which the services provided by local governments are structured

Despite the efforts in introducing the reform, according to the available empirical evidence, the systematic utilization of performance information in the budgeting process is affected by the predominance of information on inputs and, in certain cases, outputs but rarely outcomes; by the limited availability of measurable indicators; and by a rare utilization of past performance results to inform future targets (Reichard and van Helden 2020). However, some good practices have been identified (see Box 2.6).

BOX 2.6: PBB IN GERMAN LOCAL GOVERNMENTS

The city of Mannheim has been indicated as an example of a 'good practice' budget among larger German cities because it elaborates a budget that includes information on outcomes, specifically in the form of outcome targets and indicators.

The budget has a rather detailed and differentiated structure, following the prescriptions of the budget and accounting code. In particular, the budget is classified into programmes, which are divided into product groups and again subdivided into single products. For each product group, the budget indicates the total amount of revenues and expenses, the net balance, and several performance targets and indicators. For each product group, a cash flow plan and a detailed schedule of planned investments are also provided. Notably, targets and indicators elaborated with reference to product groups are focused on both outputs and, even if more limited, outcomes. For every target, the budget provides several indicators.

For example, with reference to the budget section titled 'Children, Youth, and Family' and the product group 'General youth assistance', the budget sets the following output target (website budget of 2019, https://www.mannheim.de/de/stadt-gestalten/politik/gemeinderat/haushalt-201819):

- Opportunities for and offerings of youth support and for social youth work to support people between six and 27 years of age are provided

Then, the budget establishes the following output indicators:

- Opening hours of the various youth-related activities and locations
- Number of openly accessible youth facilities
- Number of district meetings with citizens related to the project to develop the co-determination of youngsters

The outcome target for these products is established in the following manner: 'Places and offered activities of child and youth support are for all youngsters accessible, attractive, and are actively used'. Further, the budget includes the following outcome indicators:

- Number of visits in all offered services of child and youth support in municipal facilities
- Proportion of municipal schools collaborating with municipal facilities in child and youth support
- Proportion of barrier-free facilities for child and youth support (accessible for the disabled as well)

The efforts made by the local government are appreciable and indicate the increasing attention paid to measuring additional dimensions of performance, although the so-called outcome indicators show the outputs in reality.

Source: Reichard and Van Helden 2020

Although the history of performance budgeting in the Netherlands can be traced back at least 40 years, it can be labelled as a government-wide reform only within the last 20 years (de Jong et al. 2013). It was between 1999 and 2002 that the Netherlands converted to more structured forms of performance budgeting for the central administrations; earlier, the line item 'budget' included minimal performance information with no explicit and clear links between expenses and performance information. At the beginning of 2000, an ambitious budget reform was adopted with the aim of introducing a performance programme budget, whereby each ministry could allocate its expenditures according to policy goals. Compared to the former input budget, PBB was initially considered a major step forward (van Nispen and Posseth 2007). The reform was designed to integrate financial and performance planning into the annual budget cycle, thereby creating a single dominant process for both financial and performance planning (de Jong et al. 2013). According to the OECD (2007), the performance budgeting process in the Netherlands was characterized as being a comprehensive top–down and big-bang approach.

The system was further revised between 2011 and 2013 and because of the criticalities in implementing the previous reform, a more modest reform called 'accountable budgeting' was introduced (de Jong et al. 2013). This budgeting reform was designed to reduce the inclusion of performance information in the budgeting process to information that was considered useful and for which an appropriate link with resources could be established (de Jong et al. 2013). According to the new budgeting framework, quantitative performance targets can be included in the budget only if a minister can be held accountable for the results (de Jong et al. 2013). Moreover, more emphasis is placed on policy reviews for assessing effectiveness, which is in accordance with the fact that the Dutch system is characterized by multiple forms of analysis as spending reviews and policy reviews (de Jong et al. 2013).

Thus, this experience is particularly relevant because it is an example of a country that has chosen to change its strategy and adopt a more 'modest' approach to performance budgeting. If, on the one hand, this can be considered contrary to NPM logics and to the relevance of performance information, on the other hand it appears to be the result of a learning-by-doing process in which strict rules and a rigid comprehensive approach is initially adopted (de Jong et al. 2013), thereby revealing its weaknesses and making the shift possible. This change confirms that simply reporting information does not imply its effective use and not all types of performance information are relevant.

Further, ambitious budgeting reforms were also adopted at the local level of government in the Netherlands. Since the late 1980s, reforms were introduced to improve planning and control processes. The so-called policy and management instruments (PMI) project was introduced to reform policy and management instruments. It can be considered the implementation of the NPM movement at the Dutch local government level. This reform was mainly designed to (1) reinforce the position of elected politicians; (2) improve planning and control processes through the introduction of output budgeting, more cost-efficient behaviour, and high-quality information on the effects of programmes and services; and (3) strengthen customer satisfaction and effectiveness by paying more attention to customers/citizens (Reichard and van Helden 2020). A significant reform took place in 2002, when the previous structure of the budget in chapters and functions was abolished and replaced by the discretionary structure of the budget into programmes and sub-programmes (ter Bogt et al. 2015). This structure of the budget recalls the programme budget, whose aim is to support governments in defining the programmes that are required to be implemented and identify the objectives, activities, and resources required for each programme. The analysis of the implementation of reforms highlights that municipalities have adopted mandatory policy indicators, but these indicators are not always integrated into the budgetary documents, and targeting and benchmarking of performance information remain, in general, underdeveloped (Budding et al. 2019). Nevertheless, good practices have been identified (see Box 2.7).

BOX 2.7: PBB IN DUTCH LOCAL GOVERNMENTS: THE CASE OF EINDHOVEN

The budget is structured according to programmes. Eindhoven distinguishes a total of nine programmes and each programme is divided into sub-programmes. For each sub-programme, information on objectives, activities, and costs is provided. Sub-programme figures (outcome targets, output targets, costs, and revenues) are presented for the previous two years, the budget year, and the subsequent three years. Compared to other municipalities, Eindhoven links objectives, outcome targets, and output targets to create an objectives tree.

The local government utilizes the mandatory policy indicators in the budget and compares the figures with other municipalities.

For example, with reference to the sub-programme 'Youth aid', the budget has set the following objective: 'Self-reliance and social participation among youngsters'. Examples of linked outcome indicators are listed below:

- Percentage of youngsters who are aged up to 18 years with youth aid
- Percentage of youngsters with youth protection
- Percentage of youngsters with youth probation

For each of these outcome indicators, there are a few output indicators. For instance, with reference to the first outcome indicator listed above (i.e. percentage of youngsters who are aged up to 18 years with youth aid), there are the following output indicators:

- Youngsters with outpatient youth aid
- Inflow over outflow outpatient youth aid
- Youngsters with inpatient youth aid

Hence, the case of Eindhoven appears to have numerous features of an outcome-based budget. It is worth mentioning here because it performs benchmarking activities that enable a comparison of the value of outcome indicators, makes significant efforts in visualizing the linkages among objectives and targets, and elaborates on target outcome indicators and output indicators. These elements are appreciable and signal the presence of PBB, although there is still room for improvement in the elaboration of performance indicators.

Source: Reichard and van Helden 2020

2.2.5 Conclusions

To sum up the experiences previously discussed, it is possible to state that performance budgeting is still a fluctuating reform, which has been adopted and then abandoned or revised over time. The experiences in this chapter clearly point out the need for adapting the PBB reform to the specific context where it has to be implemented, leaving certain discretion to develop the processes given a general framework and certain guidelines. The Italian experience is an example of a country where the reform has been introduced by decree and in a centralized way. Its application is uniform across ministries and still partial. In this context, it has proven difficult to develop a differentiated approach to PBB according to the specific government. An improvement can be recorded with reference to performance indicators because of specific guidelines and technical work carried out to this specific purpose. Despite the improvement, performance information does not seem decisive in budgetary appropriations, while it is reported in the budgeting documents. Similarly, the use of performance information for budgeting purposes appears limited also in other countries, such as Germany and the Netherlands. A changing trajectory in PBB is visible in light of the continuous interventions and reforms concerning budgeting and performance systems. However, despite years of attempts, the most problematic part seems to be the integration of performance information in the planning phase, while it is integrated into the reporting cycle and in the policy evaluations.

References

Alach, Z. 2017. "The use of performance measurement in universities." *International Journal of Public Sector Management* 30, 2: 102–117.
Aleksandrov, E. 2020. "Actors' reflexivity and engagement in the formation of new accounting tools during university hybridization." *Qualitative Research in Accounting & Management* 17, 1:51–81.
Andersen, L.B., Boesen, A., and Pedersen, L.H. 2016. "Performance in public organizations: Clarifying the conceptual space." *Public Administration Review* 76, 6: 852–862.
Andrews, M. 2004. "Authority, acceptance, ability and performance: Based budgeting reforms." *International Journal of Public Sector Management* 17, 4: 332–344.
Anessi-Pessina, E., Barbera C., Rota S., Sicilia M., and Steccolini I.. 2016. "Public sector budgeting: A European review of accounting and public-management journals." *Accounting, Auditing & Accountability Journal* 29, 3: 491–519.
Angei, F., and Tucci, F. 2020. "Performance budgeting: un'analisi del caso italiano." *Osservatorio sui Conti Pubblici Italiani.*

Bianchi, C., and Xavier, J. A. 2017. "The design and execution of performance management systems at state level: A comparative analysis of Italy and Malaysia." *International Journal of Public Administration*, 40, 9: 744–755.

Bleyen, P., Klimovsky, D., Bouckaert, G., and Reichard, C. 2017. "Linking budgeting to results? Evidence about performance budgets in European municipalities based on a comparative analytical model." *Public Management Review* 19, 7: 932–953.

Blöndal, J.R., Kristensen, J.K., and Ruffner, M. 2003. "Budgeting in Finland." *OECD Journal on Budgeting* 2, 2: 119–152.

Blöndal, J.R., von Trapp, L., and Hammer, E. 2016. "Budgeting in Italy." *OECD Journal on Budgeting* 15, 3: 1C.

Ter Bogt, H.J., van Helden, G.J., and Kolk, B. 2015. "Challenging the NPM ideas about performance management: Selectivity and differentiation in outcome—oriented performance budgeting." *Financial Accountability & Management* 31, 3: 287–315.

Bonomi Savignon, A., Costumato, L., and Marchese, B., 2019. "Performance budgeting in context: An analysis of Italian central administrations." *Administrative Sciences* 9, 4: 79.

Borgonovi, E. 1996. *Principi e sistemi aziendali per le pubbliche amministrazioni.* Egea.

Bouckaert, G., and Halligan, J. 2008. "Comparing performance across public sectors." In *Performance Information in the Public Sector*, edited by Van Dooren, W., and Van de Walle, S., 72–93. Palgrave Macmillan.

Budding, T., Faber, B., and Vosselman, E., 2019. "Performance budgeting in the Netherlands." In *Performance-Based Budgeting in the Public Sector*, edited by De Vries, M., Nemec, J., and Špaček, D., 79–99. Palgrave Macmillan.

Caiden, N. 1998. "A new generation of budget reform." In *Taking Stock: Assessing Public Sector Reforms*, edited by Peters, G., and Savoie, D., 252–284. McGill–Queen's University Press.

Cepiku, D., Hinna, A., Scarozza, D., and Savignon, A.B., 2017. "Performance information use in public administration: an exploratory study of determinants and effects." *Journal of Management & Governance* 21, 4: 963–991.

Curristine, T. 2005. "Government performance." *OECD Journal on Budgeting* 5, 1: 127–151.

Dixon, R., Arndt, C., Mullers, M., Vakkuri, J., Engblom-Pelkkala, K., and Hood, C. 2013. "A lever for improvement or a magnet for blame? Press and political responses to international educational rankings in four EU countries." *Public Administration* 91, 2: 484–505.

Dobija, D., Górska, A.M., Grossi, G., and Strzelczyk, W. 2019. "Rational and symbolic uses of performance measurement: Experiences from Polish universities." *Accounting, Auditing & Accountability Journal* 32, 2: 782–810.

Downes, R., Moretti, D., and Nicol, S. 2017. "Budgeting and performance in the European Union", *OECD Journal on Budgeting* 17, 1: 1–60.

Espeland, W.N., and Sauder, M. 2016. *Engines of Anxiety: Academic Rankings, Reputation, and Accountability.* Russell Sage Foundation.

Ferlie, E., Musselin, C., and Andresani, G. 2008. "The steering of higher education systems: A public management perspective." *Higher Education* 56, 3: 325–348.

Gendron, Y. 2008. Constituting the academic performer: The spectre of super-ficiality and stagnation in academia. *European Accounting Review* 17, 1: 97–127.

Grossi, G., Kallio, K.M., Sargiacomo, M., and Skoog, M. 2020. "Accounting, performance management systems, and accountability changes in knowledge-intensive public organizations: A literature review and research agenda." *Accounting, Auditing and Accountability Journal* 33, 1: 256–280.

Grossi, G., Reichard, C., and Ruggiero, P. 2016. "Appropriateness and use of performance information in the budgeting process: Some experiences from German and Italian municipalities." *Public Performance & Management Review* 39, 3: 581–606.

Gruening, G. 2001. "Origin and theoretical basis of new public management." *International Public Management Journal* 4, 1: 1–25.

Gustaffson, A. 2004. *Reforming the Public Expenditure Management System: Medium-Term Expenditure Framework, Performance Management, and Fiscal Transparency.* The World Bank, Korea Development Institute.

Guthrie, J., and Neumann, R. 2007. "Economic and non-financial performance indicators in universities: The establishment of a performance-driven system for Australian higher education." *Public Management Review* 9, 2: 231–252.

van Helden, J., and Argento, D. 2020. "New development: Our hate–love relationship with publication metrics." *Public Money & Management* 40, 2: 174–177.

Helmuth, U. 2010. "Better performance with performance budgeting? Analyzing cases of success and failure in public administrations." *International Public Management Journal* 13, 4: 408– 428.

Hijal-Moghrabi, I. 2017. "The current practice of performance-based budgeting in the largest US cities: An innovation theory perspective." *Public Performance & Management Review* 40, 4: 652–675.

Ho, A.T.K. 2011. "PBB in American local governments: It's more than a management tool." *Public Administration Review* 71, 3: 391–401.

Ho, A.T.K. 2018. "From performance budgeting to performance budget management: theory and practice." *Public Administration Review* 78, 5: 748–758.

Ho, A.T.K., de Jong, M., and Zhao, Z. 2019. *Performance Budgeting Reform: Theories and International Practices.* Routledge.

Hou, Y., Lunsford, R. S., Sides, K. C., and Jones, K. A. 2011. "State performance-based budgeting in boom and bust years: An analytical framework and survey of the states." *Public Administration Review* 71, 3: 370–388.

van Houtum, H., and van Uden, A. 2020. "The autoimmunity of the modern university: How its managerialism is self-harming what it claims to protect." *Organization.* https://doi.org/10.1177/1350508420975347.

Jones, R., and Lüder, K., 2011. "The federal government of Germany's circumspection concerning accrual budgeting and accounting." *Public Money & Management* 31, 4: 265–270.

Jones, R., Lande, E., Lüder, K., and Portal, M. 2013. "A comparison of budgeting and accounting reforms in the national governments of France, Germany, the UK and the US." *Financial Accountability & Management* 29, 4: 419–441.

De Jong, M., van Beek, I., and Posthumus, R. 2013. "Introducing accountable budgeting: Lessons from a decade of performance-based budgeting in the Netherlands." *OECD Journal on Budgeting* 12, 3: 1–34.

Jordan, M.M., and Hackbart, M. 2005. "The goals and implementation success of state performance-based budgeting." *Journal of Public Budgeting, Accounting & Financial Management* 17, 4: 471.

Joyce, P.G. 2011. "The Obama administration and PBB: Building on the legacy of federal performance-informed budgeting?" *Public Administration Review* 71, 3: 356–367.

Kallio, K.M., and Kallio T.J.. 2014. "Management-by-results and performance measurement in universities: Implications for work motivation." *Studies in Higher Education* 39, 4: 574–589.

Kallio, K.M., Kallio, T.J., and Grossi, G. 2017. "Performance measurement in universities: Ambiguities in the use of quality versus quantity in performance indicators." *Public Money & Management* 37, 4: 293–300.

Kelly, J.M., 2005. "A century of public budgeting reform: The 'Key' question." *Administration & Society* 37, 1: 89–109.

Kong, D. 2005. "Performance-based budgeting: The U.S. experience." *Public Organization Review* 5, 2: 91–107.

Kurunmäki, L., Mennicken, A., and Miller, P. 2016. "Quantifying, economising, and marketising: Democratising the social sphere?." *Sociologie du travail* 58, 4: 390–402.

Liguori, M., Steccolini, I., and Rota, S. 2018. "Studying administrative reforms through textual analysis: The case of Italian central government accounting." *International Review of Administrative Sciences* 84, 2: 308–333.

Lu, E.Y., Mohr, Z., and Ho, A.T.K. 2015. "Taking stock: Assessing and improving performance budgeting theory and practice." *Public Performance & Management Review* 38, 3: 426–458.

Lu, Y., Willoughby, K., and Arnett, S. 2009. "Legislating results: Examining the Legal Foundations of PBB Systems in the States." *Public Performance & Management Review* 33, 2: 266–287.

Marcon, G. 2011. "L'evoluzione delle teorie sui processi decisionali delle amministrazioni pubbliche, premessa per l'interpretazione della riforma della contabilità." *Azienda pubblica* 3: 207–221.

Marcon, G., and Panozzo, F., 1998. "Reforming the reform: Changing roles for accounting and management in the Italian health care sector." *European Accounting Review* 7, 2:185–208.

Martí, C. 2019. "Performance budgeting and medium-term expenditure frameworks: A comparison in OECD Central Governments." *Journal of Comparative Policy Analysis: Research and Practice* 21, 4: 313–331.

Martin, L.L. 1997. "Outcome budgeting: A new entrepreneurial approach to budgeting." *Journal of Public Budgeting, Accounting & Financial Management* 9, 1: 108–126.

Mauro, S.G., Cinquini, L., and Grossi, G. 2017. "Insights into performance-based budgeting in the public sector: A literature review and a research agenda. *Public Management Review, 19*(7), 911–93

Mauro, S.G., Cinquini, L. and Grossi, G., 2018. "External pressures and internal dynamics in the institutionalization of performance-based budgeting: An endless process?." *Public Performance & Management Review* 41, 2: 224–252.

Mauro, S.G., Cinquini, L., and Sinervo, L.M. 2019. "Actors' dynamics toward performance-based budgeting: A mix of change and stability?." *Journal of Public Budgeting, Accounting & Financial Management* 31, 2: 158–177.

Melkers, J.E., and K. Willoughby. 2001. "Budgeters' views of state performance-budgeting systems: Distinctions across branches." *Public Administration Review* 61, 1: 54–64.

Moynihan, D.P. 2005. "What do we talk about when we talk about performance? Dialogue theory and performance budgeting." *Journal of Public Administration Research & Theory* 16, 2: 151–168.

Moynihan, D., and Beazley, I. 2016. *Toward Next-Generation Performance Budgeting: Lessons from the Experiences of Seven Reforming Countries.* World Bank.

Mussari, R. 2017. "Public budgeting from a managerial perspective." In *The Routledge Handbook of Global Public Policy and Administration*, edited by Klassen, D.C., and Thomas R., 360–372. Routledge.

Mussari, R., Tranfaglia, A.E., Reichard, C., Bjorna, H., Nakrošis, V., and Bankauskaitė-Grigaliūnienė, S. 2016. "Design, trajectories of reform, and implementation of performance budgeting in local governments: A comparative study of Germany, Italy, Lithuania, and Norway." In *Local Public Sector Reforms in Times of Crisis*, edited by Kuhlmann, S., and Bouckaert, G., 101–119. Palgrave Macmillan.

Nielsen, P.A., and Baekgaard M.. 2015. "Performance information, blame avoidance, and politicians' attitudes to spending and reform: Evidence from an experiment." *Journal of Public Administration Research & Theory* 25, 2: 545–569.

Van Nispen, F.K., and Posseth, J.J. 2007. "Performance budgeting in the Netherlands." *OECD Journal on Budgeting* 6, 4: 37–62.

Nørreklit, L., Jack, L., and Nørreklit, H. 2019. "Moving towards digital governance of university scholars: Instigating a post-truth university culture." *Journal of Management & Governance* 23, 4: 869–899.

OECD (Organisation for Economic Co-operation and Development). 2007. *Performance Budgeting in OECD Countries.* OECD Publishing.

OECD (Organisation for Economic Co-operation and Development). 2019. *Budgeting and Public Expenditures in OECD Countries 2019.* OECD Publishing.

Ongaro, E., and Valotti, G. 2008. "Public management reform in Italy: Explaining the implementation gap." *International Journal of Public Sector Management* 21, 2: 174–204.

Panozzo, F. 2000. "Management by decree. Paradoxes in the reform of the Italian public sector." *Scandinavian Journal of Management* 16, 357–373.

Parker, L.D. 2002. "It's been a pleasure doing business with you: A strategic analysis and critique of university change management." *Critical Perspectives on Accounting* 13, 5–6: 603–619.

Pianezzi, D., Nørreklit, H., and Cinquini, L. 2019. "Academia after virtue? An inquiry into the moral character (s) of academics." *Journal of Business Ethics* 167: 571–588.

Pitsvada, B., and LoStracco, F. 2002. "Performance budgeting: The next budgetary answer. But what is the question?" *Journal of Public Budgeting, Accounting and Financial Management* 14, 1: 53–73.

Pollitt, C., and Bouckaert, G. 2011. *Public Management Reform: A Comparative Analysis of NPM, the Neo-Weberian State, and New Public Governance.* Oxford University Press.

Ranalli, F., and Giosi, A. 2011. "New perspectives on budgeting procedures in Italy." *International Journal of Public Administration* 34, 1–2: 32–42.

Rebora, G., Ruffini, R., and Turri, M. 2017. "A serious game: Performance management in Italian ministries." *International Journal of Public Administration* 40, 9: 770–779.

Reichard, C., and van Helden, J. 2020. "Outcome-based performance budgeting in German and Dutch local government." In *Public Sector Reform and Performance Management in Developed Economies: Outcomes-Based Approaches in Practice,* edited by Hoque, Z. Routledge.

Reichard, C., and Küchler-Stahn, N. 2019. "Performance budgeting in Germany, Austria and Switzerland." In *Performance-Based Budgeting in the Public Sector* (pp. 101–124). Palgrave Macmillan.

Robinson, M., and Brumby, J. 2005. *Does Performance Budgeting Work? An Analytical Review of the Empirical Literature.* Working Paper No. 5-210. International Monetary Fund.

Salminen, M., and Viitala, M. L. 2006. *Handbook on Performance Management, Governance and Accountability*, 2/2006. Ministry of Finance.

Schick, A. 1983. "Incremental budgeting in a decremental age." *Policy Sciences* 16, 1: 1–25.

Schick, A. 2003. "The performing state: Reflection on an idea whose time has come but whose implementation has not." *OECD Journal on Budgeting* 3, 2: 71–103.

Schick, A. 2014. "The metamorphoses of performance budgeting." *OECD Journal on Budgeting* 13: 2.

Servizio del Bilancio del Senato. 2007. *La classificazione del bilancio per programmi e missioni. Elementi di documentazione* (No. 11). XV Legislatura.

Sterck, M. 2007. "The impact of performance budgeting on the role of the legislature: A four-country study." *International Review of Administrative Sciences* 73, 2: 189–203.

Talbot, C. 2010. *Theories of Performance: Organizational and Service Improvement in the Public Domain.* Oxford University Press.

Thompson, F. 1994. "Mission-driven, results-oriented budgeting: Fiscal administration and the new public management." *Public Budgeting & Finance* 14, 3: 90–105.

Verbeeten, F.H. 2008. "Performance management practices in public sector organizations: Impact on performance." *Accounting, Auditing & Accountability Journal* 21, 3: 427–454.

De Vries, M., Nemec, J., and Špaček, D. 2019. *Performance-Based Budgeting in the Public Sector*. Palgrave Macmillan.

Wang, X. 2000. "Performance measurement in budgeting: A study of county governments." *Public Budgeting and Finance* 20, 3: 102–118.

Wildavsky, A. 1964. *Politics of the Budgetary Process*. Boston: Little, Brown & Co.

Wildavsky, A. 1978. "A budget for all seasons? Why the traditional budget lasts." *Public Administration Review* 38, 6: 501–509.

Wilks, S. 1995. "Reform of the national budget process in Sweden." *International Journal of Public Sector Management* 8, 2: 33–43.

3 A post-NPM era

New Public Governance and Public Value

3.1 New Public Governance

After a decade from when the paradigmatic definition of NPM was introduced, in 2006 Osborne illustrates the paradigm of New Public Governance (NPG) as a potential alternative discourse, which is distinct from NPM. NPG is a 'new orchestration of public policy implementation and public service delivery' (Osborne 2010, 7). As the name itself reveals, in this concept, the focus shifts from management to governance. This latter term is not new, but it has been significantly revised in the spirit of this paradigm. According to NPG, both a plural and a pluralist state are proposed. The plural state refers to multiple actors interdependently linked amongst each other, and a pluralist state refers to the multiple processes that characterize the policymaking system (Osborne 2006, 2010).

In the past, according to the public administration (PA) paradigm, the prevalent idea was one of a unitary state and of hierarchy as the key governance structure. Then, in the spirit of NPM, the idea of a disaggregated state – where policymaking and implementation were detached and the implementation of policies was realized through independent service providers – became a predominant idea. With the NPM, public services began to be delivered not only by governments and the public sector, as strictly intended, but also by private sector organizations and community organizations through contracts; this caused governments to become more fragmented (Dickinson 2016). This fragmentation has increased over time and has become visible in the growing creation of networks that incorporate the public, private, and voluntary sectors (Bevir and Rhodes 2011). The fragmentation in the planning and delivery of public services has resulted in the growing relevance of networks. The NPG paradigm can be contextualized on the basis of this path. Its key starting point is that efficiency and effectiveness in the delivery of public services can be achieved through reliance on requisite competencies, which can be identified beyond the boundaries of public administrations. This does not necessarily imply the outsourcing of activities and tasks, but it likely calls for the establishment of networks of public, private, and third-sector organizations and partnerships with citizens.

The theoretical background of NPG can be found in organizational sociology and the network theory (Osborne 2006). The key result of collaborations is the exchange of ideas and resources to enhance effective and democratic governance, the facilitation of governance, and the development of innovative solutions (Torfing and Triantafillou 2013). Accordingly, the key features of NPG are represented by the revision of public service planning and delivery arrangements and the revisions of governance to enhance collaborations. One of the key expectations of NPG is to increase efficiency and effectiveness by relying on participatory mechanisms (Voorberg et al. 2015) while maintaining traditional public values and preventing the unintended effects of the managerial orientation of NPM. The forms of partnerships with non-governmental actors based on contractual arrangements that were inspired by NPM and worked under competition as the leading principle were replaced by non-competitive contractual partnerships: Rather than focusing on agencification, competition, and choice, the NPG focuses on coordination, participation, and co-production (Osborne 2010; Wiesel and Modell 2014). First, the focus shifted from centralized control, legality, and compliance, to intra-organizational processes, management, efficiency, and economy; thereafter, it shifted to effectiveness, inter-organizational relationships, and the governance of processes. Ultimately, it became evident that the elements of NPG, NPM, and PA can co-exist and produce different hybrids and multiple tensions (Christensen and Laegrid 2010; Torfing and Triantafillou 2013).

The revision of governance logics and arrangements is one of the key components of NPG. This occurs at different levels. The first level concerns the establishment of new collaborative mechanisms among organizations. In this case, inter-organizational and network management (e.g., networks or public–private partnerships) occur when people act as representatives of their organizations. The second level introduces new collaborative mechanisms between governments and citizens. In this case, extra-organizational management occurs when people who are representing an organization (e.g., government professionals) collaborate with people who do not belong to any specific organization, such as in the case of co-production of public services (Sancino and Jacklin-Jarvis 2016). In this latter regard, the reforms follow an incremental path of changes, which range from a unidirectional approach (sharing of information) to an interactive stage that is built on the participation of stakeholders, thereby shifting from responsiveness to collaboration (Vigoda 2002).

The conceptual re-elaborations of governance have flourished in this context inspired by NPG. New forms of governance arise where the government is not necessarily the centre of service delivery and multiple actors contribute to the delivery of public services (Bevir and Rhodes 2011). Several ideas have been developed such as the concepts of network governance, collaborative governance, and the idea of a new form of governance 'without government' where governance is intended as the machinery of self-organizing inter-organizational networks which function both with and without government to provide public services through interdependent networks, with significant autonomy from the state (Emerson et al. 2012; Kickert 1993; Rhodes 1996; Stoker 2006). Another perspective discusses the idea of decentred governance, according to which what is important is the understanding and meanings attached by individuals to actions, practices, and institutions (Rhodes 2007). According to NPG, governance involves self-regulation, but collaboration is more important in order to deliver effective, democratic, and innovative solutions (Torfing and Triantafillou 2013). Thus, the ambition of the paradigm becomes to enable the governance of governance, thereby leading to governance being defined as a third-order activity or metagovernance (Kooiman 2003; Torfing and Triantafillou 2013).

Therefore, we can claim that the idea of consumerism has expanded from NPM to involve arrangements that differ from market-like arrangements, thereby resulting in hybrid forms of governance (Fotaki 2011). In this regard, the idea of governance logics has emerged to explain the variation in public governance practices (Lynn et al. 2000). Hybridization can be defined as the process through which elements of diverse governance logics are integrated into context-specific configurations of governance practices (Wiesel and Modell 2014). The new governance mechanisms and practices emerge in the context of older governance modes and this leads to complex, hybrid practices (Koppenjan and Koliba 2013).

In this new system of governance arrangements, accountability relationships are also re-shaped to involve not only political and constitutional accountabilities but also to require a variety of horizontal and diagonal accountability procedures and mechanisms to manage the new relationships with citizens and private and third-sector organizations (Grossi and Thomasson 2015; Torfing and Triantafillou 2013). The state may maintain the steering role but softer tools and policy instruments may be implemented as part of the new governance arrangements (Dickinson 2016). Given this multiplicity of actors, additional elements that have assumed growing relevance within NPG are trust, relational capital, and relational contracts (Bovaird 2006). Indeed, the way in which actors interact influences their perceptions about the process of engagement and the consequent results (Källström et al. 2020).

In this new context, there is a difference in the types of performance indicators adopted, the design of performance information systems, and their use (Van Helden et al. 2012). In the case of multi-actor collaborations and networks, information is expected to be mainly used to support debate and dialogue among partners (Almqvist et al. 2013). Further, the accounting and reporting systems are reshaped in line with the development of networks and the broadening of government boundaries. An example is represented by the focus on whole-of-government accounting and consolidation (Grossi et al. 2009) and the development of social and sustainability reporting (Manes Rossi et al. 2020).

To sum up the review of the key concepts of NPG (see Box 3.1), as with previous paradigms, it is possible to claim that although there is no unique shared conceptualization of NPG, it is possible to converge on key principles and elements that are common to the different practices and reforms inspired by NPG. The following box summarizes the key elements of NPG.

BOX 3.1: THE ELEMENTS OF NPG

According to the review on the topic, it can be assumed that NPG is based on an outward orientation rather than an inward one, with an emphasis on the role played by civic society, communities, and public and private actors, on the relevance of the relationship between actors and the creation of networks.

The key components of NPG can be summarized in the following manner:

- Public organizations oriented towards the external environment
    - Network governance, collaborative governance, etc.
    - Multi-actor collaboration and cooperation-based external relations
    - Empowered (citizen) participation
- Focus on effectiveness, efficiency, public service delivery, and democracy
- Multiple forms of accountability, ranging from vertical to horizontal and diagonal forms
- New tools of government and new approaches to accounting

The NPG has the potential for improving public policymaking and public service delivery through reliance on more participatory and collaborative forms of government (Agranoff and McGuire 2003), but this is not a panacea. It is strongly encouraged that a 'sober' view be adopted in order to balance the potential positive results as well as the challenges and limitations related to NPG (Torfing and Triantafillou 2013).

Each key element and principle of NPG leads to critical challenges. For example, the involvement of a multiplicity of actors requires that they are both able and willing to collaborate. This leads to problems in terms of actor involvement, as discussed in the following chapter. Further, the involvement of citizens and stakeholders must simultaneously guarantee equal participation while preserving the legal authority granted to elected politicians. Therefore, the management of collaboration calls for new and appropriate skills on the part of managers. Finally, controlling the activities performed and assessing the results achieved require flexibility in the definition of 'performance targets and standards' and indicate the need for setting shared goals and determining indicators (Torfing and Triantafillou 2013).

3.2 Public Value

In 1995, a book entitled *Creating Public Value* written by Mark Moore was published. However, at the time, the attention was mostly captured by NPM and neo-liberalism. Thereafter, the key principles inspiring the book were reconsidered and attracted growing attention among both scholars and practitioners. In 2013, Moore wrote another book entitled *Recognizing Public Value*; this further contributed to the development of this new paradigm. Thus, Public Value (PV) has been intended to be 'the next big thing in public management' (Talbot 2009, 167). Nevertheless, there is no agreement on whether or not it can be considered an appropriate paradigm. It has been considered inappropriate to define PV management as a paradigm because it has been indicated to be unable to translate problems into (proposed) solutions (Alford et al. 2017); however, others have considered it as a new paradigm, a movement, or a new narrative for networked governance (Alford and Hughes 2008; Bryson et al. 2014; O'Flynn 2007; Stoker 2006). Public management scholars and public administration researchers have given this topic significant attention and substantial theoretical work has been developed around it.

The key components of the movement have been identified in the elements mentioned below. These elements are not new per se, but their combination brings a novel perspective to addressing new and current challenges (Bryson et al. 2014):

- Emphasis on public value/public values
- Role of the government as a guarantor of public values

- Broadly conceived importance of public management
- Importance of service to and for the public
- Emphasis on citizenship and democratic and collaborative governance

As the last point suggests, a paradigm focused on public value can be considered to be linked to NPG. The PV approach recognizes that in order to fulfil the goals of public sector organizations and produce public value, public managers must engage with other actors as lawmakers, interest groups, regulators, and the general public by creating an appropriate legitimizing environment (Alford et al. 2017). Dialogue and engagement between state and civil society have been considered a defining feature of public value management (Shaw 2013). In particular, the development of a public value-focused paradigm can be justified as a response to the issues determined by NPG. As indicated in the academic debate, NPG has posed significant management challenges due to revised governance arrangements (Stoker 2006). In this vein, PV has been intended as a paradigm that may provide a framework to guide public servants in the new context of public service delivery (Bryson et al. 2014; Stoker 2006). However, the core of PV is the focus on the ends (the creation of public value) which requires the choice of the most appropriate pragmatic means according to the context (Alford and Hughes 2008).

The initial key idea at the centre of PV was that the goal of a government is to deliver public value; this idea has been symbolized by the so-called 'strategic triangle' (Moore 1995), according to which attention must be paid to the following three key issues: the public value required to be produced, the sources of legitimacy and support to be used to authorize governments to take action, and the operational capabilities required to achieve the results. The first aspect of this model is the identification of the public value that is required to be delivered. It is important to clarify the purpose that needs to be attained and make people accountable for achieving it. In an environment where people are required to act, legitimacy and support are required up to the point that the environment must enable authorization (Moore and Khagram 2004). In this context, a key role is assigned to public managers who are expected to operate within an authorizing environment, thereby involving a variety of people in different positions who can influence various other individuals in taking their decisions. In this context, the concept of organizational strategy has gained prominence (Moore and Khagram 2004).

The core concept of this paradigm is a source of ambiguities. One of the first dimensions of debate involves what public value is. It is difficult to define this ambiguous, complex, and multidimensional concept because it recalls other concepts such as the common good, public goods, and the commonwealth (Bryson et al. 2014). Recent contributors to this debate on 'what public value is' include Alford and O'Flynn (2009), Benington and Moore (2011), Moore (1995, 2013), O'Flynn (2007), Rhodes and Wanna (2007), and Stoker (2006). The difficulties in building a widespread shared meaning of 'public value' derives from the difficulties associated with appropriately defining both *public* and *value*. According to Moore (1995), the public value is consumed collectively by citizens. In this vein, it has been claimed that public services are public not on the basis of who delivers them (Alford and Hughes 2008; Stoker 2006). This approach reveals that the key factor influencing the 'publicness' of services is represented by who consumes the services rather than who produces them. This implies that public services may be delivered by a multiplicity of different actors. Second, the term 'value/values' poses additional challenges because the expression has been used both in its singular and plural forms. The two notions of value and values are closely linked although they have been discussed as separate concepts in the literature where value has its roots in classical economics and values in the fields of philosophy, ethics, society, sociology, and related areas (Talbot 2010). The idea of overarching public values or public interest (Bozeman 2007) has an extremely long history, while the idea of public value is more recent and can be linked to the work of Moore. On the one hand, for example, Bozeman discusses public values, using the plural form, and defines public values as those 'providing normative consensus about (1) the rights, benefits, and prerogatives to which citizens should (and should not) be entitled; (2) the obligations of citizens to society, the state, and one another; (3) and the principles on which governments and policies should be based' (Bozeman 2007, 13). On the other hand, Moore and numerous other scholars have used the notion of public value, in its singular form, assuming public value as an aggregate (Alford et al. 2017). Public value encompasses several dimensions of value that a democracy wishes to realize through the delivery of services. This concept must go beyond the neo-liberal preoccupation of delivering efficient services to embrace multiple aspects. Indeed, in the recognition of what must be included in the category of public value, there is the recognition that what citizens want from a government is a combined set of elements that encompass high-performing, service-oriented public bureaucracies; efficient and effective services; and justice and fairness (Moore 1995).

Public value is more than a summation of the individual preferences of the users or producers of public services. The **judgment of what is public value is** collectively built through deliberation involving elected and appointed government officials and key stakeholders. The

achievement of public value, in turn, depends on actions chosen in a reflexive manner from a range of intervention options that rely extensively on building and maintaining networks of provision.

(Stoker 2006, 42, emphasis added.)

The creation of public value is the production of what is valued by the public, what is good for the public, or what is assessed against various public value criteria (Alford and O'Flynn 2009; Benington and Moore 2011; Bryson et al. 2014; Stoker 2006). Accordingly, there must be a balance between utilitarian concerns regarding efficiency and effectiveness, which lead to questions related to satisfaction, flexibility, responsiveness, and deontological concerns (which refer to justice and fairness) (Moore 2014). This implies that the definition of value(s) and the understanding of the value creation in the context of collaborations among multiple actors and hybrid organizations become even more ambiguous and contested (Vakkuri and Johanson 2020).

A second dimension of discussion is represented by the role that public managers are expected to play in the creation of public value. Indeed, while Moore suggests that public managers must act as entrepreneurs who look to build the creation of public value, other scholars see in this the risk of compromising the role of elected politicians (Stoker 2006). Hence, PV poses questions of democratic accountability, as both public managers and elected officials are expected to deliver public value, with a focus on the final creation of public value and the guarantee that what the public desires is addressed (Bryson et al. 2014).

This paves the way to new challenging issues. Since politics and management go hand in hand, accountability is influenced accordingly (Stoker 2006). Public managers and policymakers are both expected to take key decisions and choose the appropriate tools and mechanisms to deliver public services, and create public value from among different alternatives on the basis of pragmatic criteria (Bryson et al. 2014). Various tools suggested within the PV approach, like the strategic triangle, require managers to reflect on what is desirable, what is justifiable, and what is possible in order to take their decisions (de Jong et al. 2017). For example, Moore (2014) proposes that managers examine costs and benefits and less tangible aspects when taking decisions and specifically assessing the creation of public value. In this seminal paper, Moore identified the need for a PV accounting perspective that reflects on how to account for the value created by public services and the collectively owned assets utilized in the process (money and state authority). In this latter regard, measuring performance according to PV has become more challenging than before.

As emphasized by previous paradigms, performance measurement and management systems can, in theory, function as suitable tools for evaluating the results achieved. In the context of PV, this paradigm can be considered suitable for guiding the analysis, interpretation, and assessment of the results achieved. The development of the initial idea of public value management has included a more extensive use of performance measurement systems to recognize the value created. On the one hand, this is equivalent to considering multiple dimensions and aspects of performance: The idea of public value does not include only a financial dimension; on the contrary, it also emphasizes the achievement of democratic values. On the other hand, measuring public value is a significant challenge and does not have a single solution. This is consistent with the growing awareness of the relevance of an outcome-based performance management system (Borgonovi et al. 2018) and the call for further research to address the essential lack of overall empirical research on this topic (Bracci et al. 2019).

Government managers have attempted to measure the social outcomes – which are the final outcomes of government activities but the most difficult to measure – and the satisfaction of citizens with services provided. As explicitly recognized, 'public managers have a difficult time measuring and demonstrating the value of what they are producing. This makes the problem described above – the continuing contention about whether the organization is producing something of value to diverse authorizers – even more difficult' (Moore and Khagram 2004, 8). Scholars have stated that multiple criteria may need to be utilized to 'calculate' how much public value is created (Bozeman 2007; Talbot 2010). However, it remains a big problem to develop an accounting system that is suitable for capturing and quantifying the value of what the government produces (Moore 2013). And the contribution of the accounting discipline to the topic is significantly under-developed.

The public value perspective can drive not only performance measurement and management systems but also other accounting and control processes, stimulating the development of alternative budgeting processes as public value budgeting (see Box 3.2).

BOX 3.2: PUBLIC VALUE BUDGETING

The key idea upon which public value accounting is built is that public sector organizations use money and authority to create public value. This particular aspect is marked by the precise definition, measurement, and assessment of public value. Indeed, it is problematic to assign value to the results of government activities combining the utilitarian view of efficiency and effectiveness in the use of public resources with the deontological view, for instance, aimed at guaranteeing justice in society (Moore 2014).

Although delivering public value is becoming more recognized in public sector accounting (Bryson et al. 2014; Steccolini 2019), there are still few applications of the PV paradigm to budgeting (Bracci et al. 2019; Chohan and Jacobs 2017; Douglas and Overmans 2020). A recent review of the literature has pointed out the lack of empirical research and the limited number of accounting papers on public value conceptualization, creation, and measurement processes (Bracci et al. 2019).

Then, how can public value budgeting be defined?

If the final goal of an organization is to create public value, its budget should reflect this goal. Hence, there is a need to recall the elements of Moore's triangle leading to the elaboration of a budget triangle (Bandy 2015). According to this latter approach, there are three key issues to be balanced to guarantee the justification of public money spending and delivery of public value: The level of income and borrowing that determines the capacity of managers, the planned expenditures and investments that will be used to deliver goods and services, and the approval from the highest level of governance.

According to a recent conceptualization of public value budgeting, such a practice requires coordination and integration between funds and community resources, the involvement of societal stakeholders, continuous updates to the ongoing budget and, generally, more communication (Douglas and Overmans 2020). Therefore, public value budgeting is expected to combine key elements, such as the engagement of multiple stakeholders who contribute with their resources to the delivery of public value and the constant updating and communication of budgets. Public value budgeting appears to be a co-production process between public managers, politicians, and citizens, and in this sense, it is close to the idea of participatory budgeting. However, empirical findings show that it is difficult to implement a public value approach to budgeting due to the significant differences between politicians', managers', and citizens' values. The use of public value as rhetoric is indeed a consequence of contradictory values held by the relevant actors and calls for reconciliation by politicians and public managers (Chohan and Jacobs 2017).

References

Agranoff, R., and McGuire, M. 2003. "Inside the matrix: Integrating the paradigms of intergovernmental and network management." *International Journal of Public Administration* 26, 12: 1401–1422.

Alford, J., and Hughes, O. 2008. "Public value pragmatism as the next phase of public management." *The American Review of Public Administration* 38, 2: 130–148.

Alford, J., and O'Flynn, J. 2009. "Making sense of public value: Concepts, critiques and emergent meanings." *International Journal of Public Administration* 32, 3–4: 171–191.

Alford, J., Douglas, S., Geuijen, K., and 't Hart, P. 2017. "Ventures in public value management: Introduction to the symposium." *Public Management Review* 19, 5: 589–604.

Almqvist, R., Grossi, G., van Helden, G.J., and Reichard, C. 2013. "Public sector governance and accountability." *Critical Perspectives on Accounting* 24, 7–8. 479–487.

Bandy, G. 2015. *Financial Management and Accounting in the Public Sector.* Routledge.

Benington, J., and Moore, M.H. 2011. *Public Value: Theory and Practice.* Macmillan International Higher Education.

Bevir, M., and Rhodes, R.A.W. 2011. "The stateless state." In *The SAGE Handbook of Governance*, edited by Bevir, M., 203–217. Sage Publications.

Borgonovi, E., Anessi-Pessina, E., and Bianchi, C. 2018. *Outcome-Based Performance Management in the Public Sector.* Springer.

Bovaird, T. 2006. "Developing new forms of partnership with the 'market'in the procurement of public services." *Public Administration* 84, 1: 81–102.

Bozeman, B. 2007. *Public Values and Public Interest: Counterbalancing Economic Individualism.* Georgetown University Press.

Bracci, E., Papi, L., Bigoni, M., Gagliardo, E.D., and Bruns, H.J. 2019. "Public value and public sector accounting research: A structured literature review." *Journal of Public Budgeting, Accounting & Financial Management* 31, 1: 103–136.

Bryson, J.M., Crosby, B.C., and Bloomberg, L. 2014. "Public value governance: Moving beyond traditional public administration and the new public management." *Public Administration Review* 74, 4: 445–456.

Chohan, U.W., and Jacobs, K. 2017. "Public value in politics: A legislative budget office approach." *International Journal of Public Administration* 40, 12: 1063–1073.

Christensen, T., and Lægreid, P. 2010. "Increased complexity in public organizations: The challenges of combining NPM and post-NPM." In *Governance of Public Sector Organizations* edited by Lægreid, P., and Verhoest, K. 255–275. Palgrave Macmillan.

De Jong, J., Douglas, S., Sicilia, M., Radnor, Z., Noordegraaf, M., and Debus, P. 2017. "Instruments of value: Using the analytic tools of public value theory in teaching and practice." *Public Management Review* 19, 5: 605–620.

Dickinson, H. 2016. "From new public management to new public governance: The implications for a 'new public service'." In *The Three Sector Solution: Delivering Public Policy in Collaboration with Not-for-Profits and Business*, edited by Butcher J. R., and Gilchrist D., 41–60. Australian National University Press.

Douglas, S., and Overmans, T. 2020. "Public value budgeting: Propositions for the future of budgeting." *Journal of Public Budgeting, Accounting & Financial Management* 32, 4: 623–637.

Emerson, K., Nabatchi, T., and Balogh, S. 2012. "An integrative framework for collaborative governance." *Journal of Public Administration Research & Theory* 22, 1: 1–29.

Fotaki, M. 2011. "Towards developing new partnerships in public services: Users as consumers, citizens and/or co-producers in health and social care in England and Sweden." *Public Administration* 89, 3: 933–955.

Grossi, G., and Thomasson, A. 2015. "Bridging the accountability gap in hybrid organizations: The case of Copenhagen Malmö Port." *International Review of Administrative Sciences* 81, 3: 604–620.

Grossi, G., Newberry, S., Bergmann, A., Bietenhader, D., Tagesson, T., Christiaens, J., Van Cauwenberge, P., and Rommel, J. 2009. "Theme: Whole of government accounting: International trends." *Public Money & Management* 29, 4: 209–218.

Källström, L., Mauro, S.G., Sancino, A., and Grossi, G. 2020. "The governance games of citizens and stakeholders' engagement: Longitudinal narratives." *Local Government Studies*. https://doi.org/10.1080/03003930.2020.1807340.

Kickert, W.J. 1993. "Autopoiesis and the science of (public) administration: Essence, sense and nonsense." *Organization Studies* 14, 2: 261–278.

Kooiman, J. 2003. *Governing as Governance.* SAGE.

Koppenjan, J., and Koliba, C. 2013. "Transformations towards new public governance: Can the new paradigm handle complexity?" *International Review of Public Administration* 18, 2: 1–8.

Lynn Jr, L.E., Heinrich, C.J., and Hill, C.J. 2000. "Studying governance and public management: Challenges and prospects." *Journal of Public Administration Research & Theory* 10, 2: 233–262.

Manes-Rossi, F., Nicolò, G. and Argento, D. 2020. "Non-financial reporting formats in public sector organizations: a structured literature review." *Journal of Public Budgeting, Accounting & Financial Management.*

Moore, M.H. 1995. *Creating Public Value: Strategic Management in Government.* Harvard University Press.

Moore, M.H. 2013. *Recognizing Public Value.* Harvard University Press.

Moore, M.H. 2014. "Public value accounting: Establishing the philosophical basis." *Public Administration Review* 74, 4: 465–477.

Moore, M., and Khagram, S. 2004. "On creating public value: What business might learn from government about strategic management." *Corporate Social Responsibility Initiative*, Working Paper No. 3. John F. Kennedy School of Government, Harvard University.

O'Flynn, J. 2007. "From new public management to public value: Paradigmatic change and managerial implications." *Australian Journal of Public Administration* 66, 3: 353–366.

Osborne, S.P. 2006. "The new public governance?" *Public Management Review* 8, 3: 377–387.

Osborne, S.P. 2010. "Introduction the (new) public governance: A suitable case for treatment?." In *The New Public Governance?*, edited by Osborne, S.P., 17–32. Routledge.

Rhodes, R.A.W. 1996. "The new governance: Governing without government." *Political Studies* 44, 4: 652–667.

Rhodes, R.A.W. 2007. "Understanding governance: Ten years on." *Organization Studies* 28, 8: 1243–1264.

Rhodes, R.A.W., and Wanna, J. 2007. "The limits to public value, or rescuing responsible government from the platonic guardians." *Australian Journal of Public Administration* 66, 4: 406–421.

Sancino, A., and Jacklin-Jarvis, C. 2016. "Co-production and inter-organisational collaboration in the provision of public services: A critical discussion." In *Co-production in the Public Sector* edited by Fugini, M., Bracci, E., and Sicilia, M., 13–26. Springer.

Shaw, R. 2013. "Another size fits all? Public value management and challenges for institutional design." *Public Management Review* 15, 4: 477–500.

Steccolini, I. 2019. "Accounting and the post-new public management." *Accounting, Auditing & Accountability Journal* 32, 1: 255–279.

Stoker, G. 2006. "Public value management: a new narrative for networked governance?" *American Review of Public Administration* 36, 1: 41–57.

Talbot, C. 2009. "Public value: The next "big thing" in public management?." *International Journal of Public Administration* 32, 3–4: 167–170.

Talbot, C. 2010. *Theories of Performance: Organizational & Service Improvement in the Public Domain.* Oxford University Press.

Torfing, J., and Triantafillou, P. 2013. "What's in a name? Grasping new public governance as a political-administrative system." *International Review of Public Administration* 18, 2: 9–25.

Vakkuri, J., and Johanson, J.E. 2020. *Hybrid Governance, Organisations & Society: Value Creation Perspectives.* Routledge.

Van Helden, G.J., Johnsen, Å., and Vakkuri, J. 2012. "The life-cycle approach to performance management: Implications for public management and evaluation." *Evaluation* 18, 2: 159–175.

Vigoda, E. 2002. "From responsiveness to collaboration: Governance, citizens, and the next generation of public administration." *Public Administration Review* 62, 5: 527–540.

Voorberg, W.H., Bekkers, V.J., and Tummers, L.G. 2015. "A systematic review of co-creation and co-production: Embarking on the social innovation journey." *Public Management Review* 17, 9: 1333–1357.

Wiesel, F., and Modell, S. 2014. "From new public management to new public governance? Hybridization and implications for public sector consumerism." *Financial Accountability & Management* 30, 2:175–205.

4 Empirical evidence on reforms in the post-NPM era

4.1 Performance: Empirical insights into participatory practices

4.1.1 NPG and co-production

As discussed in the previous chapter, NPG promotes the establishment of collaboration among multiple actors, thereby emphasizing the role of citizens. Consistent with these ideas, public services have been delivered through government partnerships with citizens, private and non-profit actors, and other public organizations rather than being performed only by governments (Cepiku et al. 2014; Metcalfe and Lapenta 2014; OECD 2011).

NPG-inspired reforms concern the 'steering, coordination and use of the institutional arrangements formulated in policy-making and implementation processes aimed at the collective interest in a polycentric multisectoral stakeholder context to pursue the collective interest' (Antiroikko et al. 2011, 3). The polycentric multisectoral stakeholder approach is the core of the NPG paradigm and is thus realized through the implementation of participatory practices and collaborative models of governance. The traditional arrangements in the public sector for the design and delivery of public service have been significantly reshaped by involving civil society and market actors (Hartley 2005). The revised governance arrangements in the public sector promote stakeholders and citizens' involvement in public policy and management processes (Bingham et al. 2005).

Accordingly, participation becomes one of the key aspects of contemporary governance, as stated by the European Commission (EC) (European Commission 2018), and the concept of public governance is re-designed and enriched through the creation of dialogic opportunities. Multiple labels have been coined and used to refer to governance models: multilevel, participatory, or collaborative governance (e.g. Bingham et al. 2005; Fung and Wright 2001; Storlazzi 2006). The these models of governance are built on stakeholder engagement and citizen empowerment and have reinforced their role in the management and governance of public sector organizations, despite the varied definitions and conceptualizations of these concepts.

In this context where a transition from state-focused service delivery to partnerships and networks-based service delivery occurs, the concept of co-production has been redefined and occupies a central position (Poocharoen and Ting 2015). The co-production of public services has been considered a form of governance arrangement and a collaborative management logic (Bovaird 2005; Brandsen and Pestoff 2006; Hartley 2005), which is suitable for engaging citizens in the decision-making process. Compared to NPM – which considers the citizens as consumers of public services and, hence, actors with the power and right of selecting the provider of the services – NPG adds a new level of complexity to this scenario and recognizes citizens as co-producers of the services. A new alternative to public service delivery is given to public managers in addition to existing arrangements (Alford 2009). Public service design and delivery become characterized by a new relationship between state actors (e.g. direct or indirect agents of governments serving in a professional capacity) and lay actors (e.g. members of the public), which reshapes the manner in which public services are designed, delivered, and managed (Nabatchi et al. 2017).

4.1.2 Co-producing public services

Elinor Ostrom coined the term 'co-production' in the 1970s; it was defined as 'the process through which inputs used to produce a good or service are contributed by individuals who are not in the same organization' (Ostrom 1996, 1073). Thus, the key conceptual component of this practice is represented by the contribution provided to service delivery by multiple individuals who represent potentially different interests and bring diverse values. Co-production does not involve only consumers of services. According to the following definition elaborated by the Organisation for Economic Co-operation and Development (OECD), co-production indicates 'collaborative approaches where citizens or service users engage in partnerships with service professionals in the design and delivery of a public service' (OECD 2011, 27). This approach makes explicit the reference to the involvement of citizens' or users' service and their collaboration with government actors. As further explicated, co-production is 'a way of planning, designing, delivering and evaluating public services which draws on direct input from citizens, service users and civil society organizations' (OECD 2011, 32). In their multiple roles as consumers, service users, volunteers, government officials, officials acting by mandate of government, and/or officials of third-sector organizations, citizens have a new position in the delivery of public services.

The concept of co-production has been investigated from public administration and service management perspectives with consequential diverse interpretation of the concept developed over time (Osborne and Strokosch 2013). Mainly referring to the public administration (e.g. Bovaird 2007; Brandsen and Honingh 2016; Brudney and England 1983; Nabatchi et al. 2017), the recognition of a broader system of actors involved in the co-production of public services compared to traditional arrangements becomes the common trait of the varied and numerous conceptual approaches to co-production (Nabatchi et al. 2017). Therefore, co-production has been used as an umbrella concept to indicate that state actors (or state-mandated actors) and lay actors (e.g. citizens, clients, customers) work together to produce benefits throughout the public service cycle (Nabatchi et al. 2017; Verschuere et al. 2012). Specifically, the type of actors involved, the phases of the service delivery cycle when they are involved, and the type of involvement and contribution given can vary significantly. Who the co-producers are, what they co-produce, and why they produce it are key questions that make a difference among the different approaches and definitions (Alford 2014).

Co-production concerns activities that can occur at different stages of the public service cycle, such as planning, design, delivery, and evaluation (OECD 2011). Specifically, planning indicates the phase in which resources, goals, and priorities are identified and this is transformed into co-planning when such activities are performed through collaboration among stakeholders. Design indicates the phase in which activities and processes that satisfy the identified needs and priorities are defined, and it becomes a co-design phase when multiple actors contribute to it. Delivery indicates the phase whereby services are adequately (co-) delivered through the implementation of the designed activities and processes. And, finally, assessment is the phase in which public services delivered are assessed; the activities involved in this phase can also be performed by multiple stakeholders.

In addition to the different stages in which co-production can occur, it can also occur at different levels and involve different types of actors (Brudney and England 1983; Nabatchi et al. 2017). For example, it is possible to distinguish between individual, collective, and group co-production according to, for example, whether co-production involves the engagement of single individuals (individual co-production) or a specific cluster or category of lay actors sharing common needs/features (group co-production).

A further categorization and conceptualization of the phenomenon that focuses on the activities performed, the stages in the policy cycle, and the type of actors involved distinguishes between co-management, co-governance, and co-production (Brandsen and Pestoff 2006; Pestoff 2018). Co-management refers to the collaboration of third-sector organizations with the state in the production of services. Co-governance refers to the participation of third-sector organizations in the planning and delivery of services. Co-production refers to the involvement of citizens who produce their own services, at least partially.

Despite the long history of the phenomenon, co-production has assumed renewed relevance in the public sector in the wake of austerity and has been enhanced by NPG after initial interest was expressed in the 1970s and 1980s. Co-production has become a growing approach to public service delivery, as testified by the rich body of literature on the topic and the copious number of experiences in Europe. A simple form of proof of the growing interest in the practice is provided by Figure 4.1, which depicts the number of publications of different types (journal articles, proceedings, etc.) and in different languages and disciplinary fields since 1970[1]. As evident from the figure, there has been a significant increase in the number of publications over the last two decades, particularly in the last decade.

The increasing relevance of co-production is partially due to its claimed and potential benefits. Among these, the better use of resources through a more informed decision-making process and the reduction of costs are identified as potential benefits of co-production (OECD 2011), which contribute to reinforce efficiency. Further, co-producing public services can support the focus on the delivery of enhanced value, improving not only efficiency

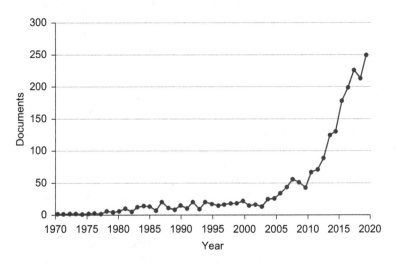

Figure 4.1 Scopus documents on co-production by year (1970–2020).

but also effectiveness (Osborne and Strokosch 2013). In this vein, the conceptualization of co-production has emphasized the production of value (Alford 2009). Public, social, and shared value may be created (Sancino 2016). Therefore, co-production can improve the quality of services and the ability to respond to citizens' needs by strengthening accountability and citizen empowerment (Boyle and Harris 2009; Ostrom 1996; Sancino 2016). In this context, it is also expected that trust and democracy are reinforced (OECD 2011). In addition to these benefits that mainly involve the actors outside the government, co-production can support the valorization of public servants' expertise (Needham 2008), thereby improving the internal management of organizations. These multiple benefits of co-production have also been analyzed through the lens of good governance, which has been considered as an overall potential outcome to be achieved through co-production (Cinquini et al. 2017; Campanale et al. 2021; OECD 2011). The complex concept of good governance includes several of the expected potential results that can be achieved through co-production, such as transparency, efficiency and effectiveness, equity, and inclusiveness.

In light of the numerous potential positive outcomes of co-production, it has become a predominant alternative to public service delivery as a suitable tool for delivering high-quality services and addressing the important challenges of public sector organizations in terms of accountability, efficiency, and effectiveness.

Further, the attention paid to co-production has enlivened numerous studies on the topic, which have investigated elements of co-production, ranging from its reasons and motivations, and roles played by state and lay actors, to difficulties related to the implementation of the practice and its consequent results, both intended and unintended (e.g. Alford 2009; Sicilia et al. 2019; Sorrentino et al. 2017; Tuurnas 2015). However, the co-production of public services cannot be considered a panacea, as it also creates multiple challenges for practitioners and may lead to disvalue rather than public value (Cluley et al. 2020).

In the case of co-produced services, tasks, responsibilities, and costs are spread over multiple actors and this implies a shift of power over multiple actors and a more complex allocation of tasks and responsibilities (Ottmann et al. 2011; Needham 2008). The boundaries of roles and responsibilities among actors become complex and blurred (Bovaird 2007; Ostrom 1996).

In this context, accountability mechanisms must be redefined (Ackerman 2004), thereby leading the way to new forms of accountability which require the management of new vertical (e.g., between citizens and governments, and between governments and third-sector organizations or other organizations involved) and horizontal (e.g., between citizens and third-sector organizations or other organizations involved) relationships among actors. On the one hand, co-production is expected to improve accountability because actors are brought closer, thereby reducing information asymmetry, aligning preferences and incentives, and improving transparency (Besley and Ghatak 2003; Pestoff 2018). On the other hand, the changing roles among actors may create problems of governability, legitimacy, and accountability (e.g. Meijer 2016). This requires new accountability relations to be appropriately managed in order to improve relationships and communication among actors. Alternative mechanisms and new concepts (e.g. vertical, horizontal, diagonal, hybrid, reciprocal, or bottom–up accountability) have been coined (Ackerman 2004; Grossi and Thomasson 2015). Indeed, if on the one hand co-production is expected to foster trust among actors, on the other hand, the opposite situation may also occur if co-production is not adequately managed (Fledderus 2015).

Further, since co-production is built on the collaborations to be established with citizens, among whom disadvantaged citizens may be included (Jakobsen and Andersen 2013), specific issues may emerge. If on the one hand, co-production is expected to improve inclusiveness and equity, on the other hand, participants must be selected according to their ability and willingness to work effectively in partnerships (Ottmann et al. 2011). The selection of actors represents a crucial and delicate issue, with reference to both state and lay actors. If participants are not able to contribute to co-production, the effectiveness of the experiences may be undermined and costs increased (OECD 2011). The involvement of citizens must not undervalue the relevance of the role played by professionals, who are required to support, encourage, and coordinate the capabilities of different actors involved (Bovaird 2007; Tuurnas 2015, 2016).

These issues call for a careful reflection on the features of co-production, since each key element of co-production is linked to potential positive outcomes and potential crucial challenges. In this context, the design of co-production becomes relevant, as shown by a recent review of the literature on the topic (Sicilia et al. 2019); this review identified several factors considered relevant to successful management of co-production, such as organizational (e.g. organizational structures and professional roles) and procedural factors (e.g. participant selection and preparation and process design). The effective management of co-production must be based on appropriately designed mechanisms, rules, and processes, which must be adapted to the local circumstances in order to guide the behaviour of actors towards the achievement of shared goals (Ottmann et al. 2011).

4.1.3 The challenge of performance measurement

The spread of co-production has emphasized the need for a shift in the measurement of performance. Since the co-production of public services is built on a stronger focus on the final aim of the activities (i.e. the delivery of services) compared to traditional approaches, it implies that greater attention should be paid to output and, especially, outcome measures. The shift from activities and outputs to outcomes has been defined as 'the core of the new paradigm offered by co-production' (OECD 2011, 29). In this context, it becomes crucial to develop an outcome-based performance management approach suitable for coping with collaborative governance (Xavier and Bianchi 2020). On the one hand, the academic debate has recognized the relevant role of outcomes in the design of co-production experiences (Campanale et al. 2021; Tuurnas 2016). On the other hand, the empirical investigation of outcome measurement and management remains limited (Boyle and Harris 2009; Brandsen and Honingh 2016; Nabatchi et al. 2017; Needham 2008; OECD 2011; Sancino 2016). The problems are multifarious (see an example in Box 4.1). First, there is a difficulty in both defining the outcomes of production and in measuring them (Cepiku et al. 2020; Voorberg et al. 2015). The definition of co-production outcomes is in itself a challenge given the multiple stakeholders involved (Cepiku et al. 2020); the different good governance principles and expectations leading the practice (Campanale et al. 2021), which makes it difficult to design a focused performance system; and the blurred boundaries among organizations, units, and levels of analysis. Outcome measurement is increasingly being recognized as a relevant dimension of performance measurement; simultaneously, it is the most challenging and the least developed. Only a few studies (e.g. Boyle and Harris 2009; Levine and Fisher 1984) have attempted to introduce performance measures, such as satisfaction measures, decreases in costs, quality measures, and output measures (e.g. an increase in the number of services). The role of co-production in improving cost efficiency has been recognized in the academic debate but it calls for further investigation in order to reflect on the direct and indirect costs of co-production: efficiency measures per sé may be not meaningful if the costs borne by citizens are not considered (Garlatti et al. 2020). Further, when multiple actors are involved, a multiplicity of values may be detected and this may result in contrasting goals and additional challenges in performance measurement since there will be the need for balancing financial and non-financial concerns (Campanale et al. 2020).

BOX 4.1: CO-PRODUCING PUBLIC SERVICES: THE ITALIAN EXPERIENCE

Co-production experiences have flourished in the fields of health and social care services. This box provides a few insights into two experiences undertaken in Italy in a regional area where several legislative interventions were taken by the regional government to support participatory and collaborative practices.

In this context, an experience of co-production is represented by the delivery of social housing services. This experience began with the establishment of an association to deal with housing problems. The association provides the services in collaboration with social service professionals; municipalities; the regional government; private, voluntary, and third-sector organizations; and users. The co-production consists of creating the opportunity to meet and satisfy the needs of those looking for houses with the needs of those seeking assistance. Indeed, citizens may share their houses with poor people in return for assistance. Alternatively, public buildings in the municipality can be identified and assigned as social houses, where citizens can live and contribute to cover the cost of utilities.

Another example of co-production of public services concerns the delivery of services to young disabled people, which began with the establishment of a foundation to support the achievement of autonomy by young disabled people and to improve the quality of their lives. The foundation provides these services in association with social and healthcare professionals, the families of young disabled people, and the municipalities. They collaborate to plan, design, and deliver personalized services, which can vary from the organization of leisure activities to the arrangement of cohabitation periods for the disabled young. The municipalities support these activities by providing financial aids and apartments.

In both cases, the association/foundation is the institutional actor that leads the process of co-production. As service users, citizens make a relevant and indispensable contribution to the design, delivery, and evaluation of public services.

Concerning the evaluation of co-produced services, citizens co-elaborate qualitative reports to illustrate the activities conducted and the results achieved. The emphasis is placed on qualitative rather than quantitative information and this is informative of the need of communicating information that is clearly understandable by users and suitable for depicting the outcome achieved rather than detailing the resources utilized and the cost incurred. These latter pieces of information are also provided, mainly for accountability purposes, to the local and regional governments. However, the main emphasis is on the call for guaranteeing responsiveness in co-production, thereby reshaping the horizontal relationships among organizations.

Despite the elaboration of detailed reports per user and the involvement of users in their elaboration, in both cases, it is possible to recognize the lack of a developed performance measurement system.

First, the role of management accountants is performed by professionals, such as sociologists and physiologists working in the foundation/association leading the co-production. Professional management accountants are not involved, and this lack of specialized knowledge and competencies may explain the difficulties faced by organizations in developing relevant performance indicators and building appropriate systems.

Second, the multiple actors involved challenge the production and interpretation of comprehensive information. Organizations that lead co-production, the professional actors involved, users, and the community require a multidimensional system. The results are influenced by all the actors involved and this would require the monitoring and measurement of the entire value chain; however, this poses additional challenges to the management of co-production.

Third, and in particular, in both cases there is the recognition of the relevance of measuring the impact of services on the well-being of users and their families and the cost savings generated by co-production for the community and the public sector. Nevertheless, in both cases, outcome and cost measures are difficult to be detected, while qualitative narrative information is produced for reporting the results achieved and the satisfaction of users.

Source: Campanale, Mauro, and Sancino 2021

4.2 Budgeting: Empirical insights into participatory budgeting

4.2.1 NPG and participatory budgeting

The adoption of the budgeting reform known as participatory budgeting has been enhanced by the development of the NPG paradigm. Although the origins of participatory budgeting can be traced back to earlier times compared to when NPG was formalized, this latter reform paradigm has supported the spread of the principles which are beyond participatory budgeting (Bingham et al. 2005). Indeed, NPG is built on the call for adopting collaborative approaches in public sector governance and involving external and internal stakeholders in policymaking and service delivery (Cepiku et al. 2014; Osborne 2006; Storlazzi 2006). NPG posits both a plural state, where multiple actors contribute to the delivery of public services, and a pluralist state, where multiple processes inform the policymaking system (Osborne 2006). In this context, the involvement of a wide set of actors in decision-making is enhanced. The role that budgeting can play in this regard is potentially relevant (Ebdon and Franklin 2006) since public budgeting is traditionally informed by negotiations among multiple actors; moreover, due to the growing relevance of the effective utilization of public funds, including citizens in such negotiations may make a difference.

The practice of participatory budgeting occurs in the broader context of reforms whereby various arrangements are established to enable different actors to participate in the planning and delivery of public services. Participatory budgeting has been considered a good example of 'co-governance for accountability' (Ackerman 2004) and of 'co-production' since citizens are involved in joint decision-making processes related to resource allocation (Barbera et al. 2016) with the purpose of strengthening accountability.

4.2.2 Insights into participatory budgeting: A label for multiple logics?

Since the 1980s, the accounting practice of participatory budgeting has received growing recognition among scholars, practitioners, and policy-makers with a steady increase in attention over the last 30 years (Bartocci et al. 2021). The term *participatory budgeting* refers to the practice of involving unelected citizens in the budgeting process and specifically in the allocation of public resources. This budgeting practice is built on the active participation of citizens in budgetary decisions.

The depth of participatory budgeting may be assessed based on the manner in which citizen participation is framed. It is well accepted that 'participation of the governed in their government is, in theory, the cornerstone of democracy' (Arnstein 1969, 216). However, how it is translated into practice is a challenge. Participation may range from being symbolic to involving a large and diverse group of citizens, whereby citizens are engaged in meaningful discourse with governments (Fung 2006). The scope of participation can vary on a ladder of eight levels according to the well-known elaboration given by Arnstein (1969) – ranging from manipulation (the lowest level of the ladder) to citizen control (the highest level of the ladder). Citizens may be simply consulted or empowered to make their voices heard and influence governmental decisions. The extent to which participatory practices such as participatory budgeting may be implemented is influenced by the approaches beyond them and the manner in which the participation of citizens is set out to be.

Participatory democracy and deliberative democracy, despite being differently interpreted, have been the two main basic theoretical frameworks that have inspired the research and work on participatory budgeting (Sintomer et al. 2008). Participatory democracy considers the engagement of citizens as a means to empower them and make their voices heard. This is extremely important in less developed countries where political and economic systems may be less developed (de Sousa Santos 1998). Deliberative democracy emphasizes the pluralist state where citizen participation in the budgeting process requires the establishment of a dialogue among citizens to find agreement on what to do (Bobbio 2019). This implies the relevance of creating a dialogue among actors. This assumes special relevance with reference to accounting tools in the public sector, since they cannot and must not represent only one dominant voice (particularly in the public sector) but rather encourage dialogue among multiple actors (Brown and Dillard 2015). In this vein, participatory budgeting has been considered a dialogic accounting tool (Aleksandrov et al. 2018; Mauro et al. 2020) focusing on fulfilling a broad set of values and interests (Brown and Dillard 2015). A potential interpretation of participatory budgeting as a dialogic accounting tool to create new opportunities for stakeholders, whose views are usually ignored or under-represented (Brown and Dillard 2015), is built on the stakeholder involvement in the budgeting process.

Accordingly, based on the initial prevalent conception of participatory budgeting, it has been considered a suitable tool for addressing the legitimacy crisis of representative democracy by improving the authentic involvement of the public in decision-making. In particular, this can be explained by reflecting on its origins in Brazil, where politics was characterized by patronage practices, social exclusion, corruption, and clientelism; therefore, NGOs, social movements, and numerous governments shifted to participatory budgeting ideas in order to enrich the local democracy (Shah 2019). Indeed, one of the most well-known experiences of participatory budgeting that has been considered as the starting point for its development across countries is the experience in Porto Alegre, Brazil at the end of the 1980s (Sintomer et al. 2008; Wampler 2000, 2010) (see Box 4.2), although budget participation has a longer history in the United States in broader forms than the current interpretation of participatory budget (Bartocci et al. 2021).

BOX 4.2: THE EXPERIENCE OF PORTO ALEGRE

Participatory budgeting was initiated in 1989 in the municipality of Porto Alegre, a city with over one million inhabitants. In 1988, a progressive political party won the mayoral election by promoting democratic participation. In this context, participatory budgeting was promoted in an attempt to cope with financial constraints and spending revisions. It followed an incremental path and shifted from less than 1,000 citizens who were part of the process in the first two years of adoption to over 20,000 in 1992, after only a few years of its introduction.

Participatory budgeting in Porto Alegre was implemented through a series of public meetings organized by region. Representatives of the local government and of the community (e.g. neighbourhood associations and youth clubs) are part of all meetings. In addition, the representatives of the community who act as delegates of the citizens also join the meetings to illustrate the needs of the community and discuss the setting of priorities for informing budgeting decisions.

The citizen delegates are selected to represent each region at the municipal budget council, called the Participatory Budgeting Council, along with union representatives, representatives from the union of neighbourhood associations, and representatives of central municipal agencies. The council organizes several meetings and develops a set of proposals that are then delivered to the mayor. The mayor can accept the budget or ask the council for revisions. The council may override the request with a two-thirds majority. Then, the mayor's office incorporates the proposals in its proposed budget. Thereafter, the mayor presents the budget to the local legislature, which usually approves it.

According to this approach, the final budget approved by the legislature is expected to be the result of a process of negotiation and discussions to which both government actors and unelected citizens have contributed.

Source: Fung and Wright 2001; Shah 2019

The adoption of participatory budgeting in a developing country has motivated the adoption of the practice in other developing countries other than developed countries. Thus, the case of Porto Alegre has been considered a reference model for participatory budgeting (Sintomer et al. 2008), with local variations across the world as a consequence of its widespread adoption. Currently, a great degree of diversity is evident in the adoption of participatory budgeting, since the practice has evolved through the continuous experimentation of the concept across countries, such as in Europe, America, and Asia (Shah 2019; Uddin et al. 2017).

As is often the case with long-lasting reforms, the adoption of participatory budgeting has resulted in the spread of multiple interpretations and models of the practice across contexts. The spread of the participatory budgeting approach across borders has paved the way for its differentiated conceptualization and implementation (Ganuza and Baiocchi 2012; Sintomer et al. 2008). Nowadays, there is no unique and widely accepted definition of participatory budgeting. Nevertheless, constant efforts have been made to define participatory budgeting and identify the key elements that signal the existence of participatory budgeting. An ideal version of participatory budgeting must include useful data on citizens' views regarding budget priorities, their deliberation, increased knowledge, and effective results since the decisions taken must also be implemented (Shah 2019). Frameworks and models that attempt to frame key dimensions and issues of participatory budgeting have been elaborated (Ebdon and Franklin 2006; Sintomer et al. 2008). Specifically, five criteria have been expounded to define PB (Sintomer et al. 2008):

• The budgetary dimensions must be discussed
• Governmental and non-governmental actors must be involved
• It must be an iterative process, not a single meeting
• Forms of public deliberation within the framework of specific meetings/forums are required
• Some form of accountability on outputs is required

The translation of these criteria into practice can vary due to the lack of standardized rules (Bassoli 2012; Russo 2013). A significant set of previous studies on the topic has analyzed how PB can be adopted.

First, contextual variables have been demonstrated to influence the design and adoption of participatory budgeting, such as legal, social, political, and historical contexts and local cultural conditions (Ebdon and Franklin 2006; Soguel et al. 2020; Uddin et al. 2017). Thus, the environment is one of the key variables to influence participatory budgeting. Further, previous studies have investigated the factors that influence the success of participatory budgeting (e.g. Barbera et al. 2016; Beckett and King 2002; Ebdon and Franklin 2004) – for example, strong mayoral support, a generally supportive political environment, a civil society willing to contribute to ongoing debates, and the availability of financial resources to fund projects selected by citizens (Shah 2019). Both the external environment and internal environment influence the success of participatory budgeting.

Second, participatory budgeting is a complex process whose design requires the definition of timing, the type of participants who must be involved, and types of budget allocations. Indeed, when to involve citizens and how to select citizens who must be involved are two key elements that

Figure 4.2 The budgeting process.

may define the differences among the various types of participatory budgeting. Concerning the definition of timing, it is important to take into account that participatory budgeting can influence different phases of the budgeting process, which is depicted in Figure 4.2.

The first phase involves the preparation of the budget (executive preparation), the second phase involves the legislative review and approval of the budget (legislative review), the third phase is the implementation of the budget (execution), and the fourth phase involves the evaluation and audit of the budget (audit). According to participatory budgeting, citizens may be involved in various phases of the budgeting cycle. First, and in particular, citizens are usually expected to be involved in budget preparation in order to influence the decisions on the budget. Further, there is room for involving citizens in other phases of the budgeting cycle, for example, in the evaluation phase, when spending is audited to guarantee that resources are spent in accordance with intention. Given the reform of the budget process and the wider space assigned to the evaluation of outputs and outcomes, there is more room for involving citizens as well in this phase of the budget.

Concerning the types of budget allocation, following the Porto Alegre model, participatory budgeting is usually based on the allocation of a small part of the budget according to citizens' preferences (Rubin and Ebdon 2020).

In addition, the participation and involvement of citizens in the budgeting process may be realized through the use of different mechanisms, such as public meetings, focus groups, committees, and surveys (Ebdon and Franklin 2006).

Beyond the origins of participatory budgeting, several different reasons for its adoption may be identified. There are several expectations toward participatory budgeting. In this vein, participatory budgeting has been justified in political terms since it has been viewed as a potential tool for strengthening transparency, democracy, and emancipation (Brun-Martos and Lapsley 2017; Célérier and Botey 2015). This has resulted in normative expectations regarding the potential ability of participatory budgeting to renew democracy, improve governmental decision-making, legitimize government decisions, increase transparency, and enhance citizens' trust in the government (Lerner 2011). Therefore, politicians may be interested in participatory budgeting because it can increase the likelihood of re-election (Berner et al. 2011), which may be employed as a reputational tool. Moreover, citizens may be willing to participate in this practice because they can be empowered and become aware of their rights and duties. Participatory budgeting becomes a school of citizenship and citizens learn how to negotiate and contribute to the definition of policy priorities (Shah 2019). From this perspective, a political logic beyond participatory budgeting is evident. Further, participatory budgeting can be considered a useful approach for improving the effective management of public resources (Cabannes and Lipietz 2018; de Sousa Santos 1998) and delivering better services. A managerial logic can be detected in the improved use of resources. In addition, participatory budgeting may be guided by a community-building logic, as it reinforces the connection among community groups (Lerner 2011). Therefore, political, managerial, and social expectations have been historically and widely set in connection with participatory budgeting. The various expectations – along with the diversity of actors promoting the reform (who), goals pursued (why), and design of the reform (how) – make it possible to identify three different logics – political, managerial, and community-building – that inspire participatory budgeting (Bartocci et al. 2019). The three logics can coexist or create a hybrid combination in the form of blending or layering (Bartocci et al. 2019), thereby resulting in empirical experiences which include a few elements of each logic. In fact, according to Cabannes and Lipietz (2018), the different logics that can underpin participatory budgeting are not mutually exclusive. They can, and do, coexist (Figure 4.3). In this vein, participatory budgeting must achieve a compromise between diverse values and expectations, thereby balancing and mediating different logics and silos (Brun-Martos and Lapsley 2017).

The high expectations from participatory budgeting have not always been met in practice (Ebdon and Franklin 2006; Rossmann and Shanahan 2012). A struggle between the need for new approaches to accounting, like

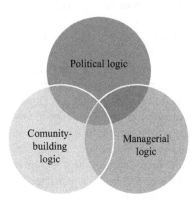

Figure 4.3 The logics of participatory budgeting.

participatory budgeting, that can facilitate participatory forms of organization, and the recognition of the limitations of participatory budgeting in achieving its expectations (e.g., Ganuza and Baiocchi, 2012; Uddin et al. 2017) has enlivened the academic debate on budgeting reforms. More recently, studies on the practice have revealed its weaknesses and controversial aspects (Ebdon and Franklin 2006; Sintomer et al. 2008; Uddin et al. 2017).

First, participatory budgeting is expected to enable stakeholders to join the debate, taking their interests, values, and expectations into account. This poses the first significant challenge: Harmonizing and balancing different interests and logics. The latter can significantly change across actors, where, for example, governments may be interested in achieving political support and promoting transparency, while citizens can be motivated by gaining access to public decision-making activities and information (Shah 2007). Thus, different interests result in different interpretations of what can be defined as effective participation (Berner et al. 2011).

Second, the representativeness is also limited by nature. Even when citizens participate actively and effectively in the budgeting process, participatory budgeting may legitimize individuals over democracy, as not all individuals are involved in the process (Michels 2011). Although it provides data on citizens' requirements, these data cannot be considered representative of the community as a whole. However, participatory budgeting may not be representative but may provide an opportunity to reveal the role of citizens (Wampler 2010).

Third, changing the power relations among actors can be a struggle and the participation of citizens may be limited compared to the key roles played by councillors and budget administrators (Uddin et al. 2017). The related risk is that participatory budgeting has no impact on the budget (Beckett and King 2002) and functions as a mechanism for increasing the power of the political elite (Célérier and Botey 2015; Uddin et al. 2011). This budgeting practice may be consultative, become a new form of domination (Ganuza and Baiocchi 2012), or end up being a monologic procedure (Aleksandrov et al. 2018) rather than a dialogic tool.

Fourth, several technical challenges limit the implementation of participatory budgeting. Public engagement activities can be time-consuming and expensive. The late or superficial engagement of citizens in the budgeting process (Yang and Callahan 2007) can hinder participatory budgeting, while it may be advisable that participation is open to a large number of people (Ebdon and Franklin 2006) and based on their early involvement. Further, the technicalities of the budgeting process can limit the contributions of citizens (Beckett and King 2002).

Therefore, the results of participatory budgeting may be disappointing, resulting in low and unrepresentative participation (Ebdon and Franklin 2006). There have also been positive experiences, but the results must not be taken for granted; it is necessary that a careful assessment of the experiences is conducted to distinguish participatory budgeting from advertising campaigns (Sintomer et al. 2008).

4.2.3 Empirical insights into participatory budgeting: The Italian case

Italy is among the first adopters of participatory budgeting in Europe and it presents an interesting pattern of diffusion, with multiple waves of development (Bartocci et al. 2016; Bartocci et al. 2019; Bassoli 2012; Russo 2013; Sintomer and Allegretti 2009). Several reforms introduced by the government in Italy required the sharing of information with the public, but this has not necessarily resulted in participative democracy or meaningful changes to decision-making (Manes Rossi and Aversano 2015). Growing pressures to increase transparency and accountability have pushed the adoption of further reforms designed to strengthen citizen engagement in the work of the government. In this vein, the adoption of participatory approaches has followed an incremental path, whereby citizens have been initially informed of government decisions and then consulted and finally involved in decision-making processes.

Further, the development of participatory budgeting was supported by several legislative interventions at the national and regional levels (Bartocci et al. 2016) and the experiences with participatory budgeting flourished, particularly at the local level of government (Allegretti and Herzberg 2004;

Russo 2013). By its nature, the local level of government is the one that facilitates the dialogue between the government and unelected citizens.

Among the first adopters of participatory budgeting in Italy was a small city in the South of Italy, the municipality of Grottammare, which introduced this reform in the 1990s, followed by several other examples (Bartocci et al. 2019; Russo 2013; Sintomer et al. 2008).

The following box (Box 4.3) illustrates a more recent experience with participatory budgeting at the local level of government in north Italy.

BOX 4.3: PARTICIPATORY BUDGETING: THE ITALIAN EXPERIENCE

A local municipality in north Italy adopted participatory budgeting in 2016. A key role was played by politicians who promoted the initiative and external experts who provided their professional support to design the practice. The idea of participatory budgeting was then divulged to the public through several public meetings, which represented a suitable environment for information sharing.

The project of adopting participatory budgeting entailed an allocation of a total budget of €160,000. These resources were expected to be used to finance projects proposed by citizens. Citizens were asked to propose ideas regarding how they would use the available funds by elaborating and submitting their projects, prepared individually or in a team. The projects concerned one of the following eight thematic areas identified by the government: (1) jobs; (2) schools; (3) public services; (4) sustainability; (5) smart city and innovation; (6) quality of space and infrastructure; (7) culture, tourism, and sport; and (8) peaceful environment. Citizens were supported by the local government in the preparation of their projects. In particular, neighbourhood associations, a specific intersectoral working group coordinated from the municipal office, and a cooperative working under its authority helped the citizens in the preparation of the required documentation. Several training meetings were also arranged to explain how to correctly write down the projects.

Thereafter, the local government analyzed the projects submitted by citizens and selected those that were considered technically and legally feasible, within an adequate and reasonable timeframe, with an accurate cost estimation, a sound local impact, and alignment with the other projects and initiatives of the municipality (a total of 24 projects). These projects were published on an online platform and on the website of the local government. Citizens were asked to vote for the project they preferred; ultimately, the most voted project in each neighbourhood was selected and allocated an amount of €20,000 in order to achieve the stated project goals. The following figure summarizes the different steps of the project (Figure 4.4).

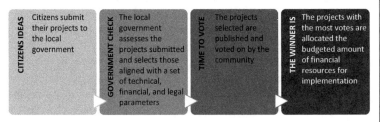

Figure 4.4 Participatory budgeting: The project.

The key points of this experience can be summarized in the following manner:

1. In addition to politicians and managers, the design and implementation of the project were supported by external experts and collaborators as well as an internal working group.
2. Citizens were involved early in the budgeting process, specifically in the phase of budget formulation (Yang and Callahan 2007), advancing their proposals rather than expressing opinions on government proposals (Allegretti and Herzberg 2004).
3. The participation was not limited to specific groups of citizens/interests, but the entire community had the opportunity of advancing proposals and/or voting for others' proposals in order to guarantee inclusiveness (Barbera et al. 2016).
4. The participation of citizens was facilitated by the use of social media platforms and online tools.
5. The participation was arranged to be both territorial and thematic (Cabannes and Lipietz 2018): A project was selected for each neighbourhood and linked to a specific predetermined theme.

The limitations and challenges are as follows:

1. The influence exercised by citizens concerned only a limited part of the budget.
2. Citizens had high expectations regarding their involvement in the budgeting process, but government actors continued to play a dominant role in budget implementation (Uddin et al. 2017).

3. Government actors and unelected citizens exchanged information, but there was no adequate dialogue among them.
4. Different forms of debate emerged, both internally – among local government actors to select the feasible projects to be voted on – and externally – among unelected citizens in designing their projects; the social relationships among unelected citizens (Lerner 2011) supported their collaboration efforts in developing the projects.
5. The accountability mechanisms do not appear to have been revised: It is not evident whether unelected citizens have been made accountable for their projects or whether government actors have held citizens accountable for the outputs achieved.
6. Communication with the government was supported by digital technologies and social media platforms, but it was not clear in terms of all the aspects. The lack of adequate communication negatively influenced the experiences of the citizens.
7. The strong separation between the planning phase and the implementation phase influenced the relationship between the government and unelected citizens. Citizens were satisfied with the planning phase, trying to influence certain budgetary decisions. Then, an actual and effective dialogue with the government was absent, limiting the success of the initiative.

Source: Mauro, Rainero, and Culasso 2020

The case illustrated in the box is an example of participatory budgeting which has been designed with the support of experts in a top–down manner. Despite being promising in theory, in practice, there is the risk that it becomes similar to an 'idea contest' rather than participatory budgeting. Nevertheless, the important experience previously discussed is useful because it enables the identification of important issues. First, participatory budgeting can potentially be a dialogic tool that is suitable for creating a dialogue among actors; however, in practice, it can become a hybrid procedure with a mixture of monologic and dialogic elements (Mauro et al. 2020). The experience of Italy discussed in the box reveals also the relevance of the choice of the forum which enables a dialogue between the government and its citizens and not simply among citizens or not merely for an exchange of preliminary information. Further, in order to make participatory budgeting work as a dialogic accounting tool, it is crucial to set proper communication channels and identify accountability mechanisms that take into account the mutual relationships among actors.

Note

1 The elaboration was conducted on Scopus by searching for documents with the keyword 'co-production' in the title, abstract, or keywords. This elaboration serves the singular purpose of providing an indication of the growing interest in the practice.

References

Ackerman, J. 2004. "Co-governance for accountability: Beyond "exit" and "voice"." *World Development* 32, 3: 447–463.

Aleksandrov, E., Bourmistrov, A., and Grossi, G. 2018. "Participatory budgeting as a form of dialogic accounting in Russia." *Accounting, Auditing & Accountability Journal* 31, 4: 1098–1123.

Alford, J. 2009. *Engaging Public Sector Clients: From Service-Delivery to Co-Production*. Palgrave Macmillan.

Alford, J. 2014. "The multiple facets of co-production: Building on the work of Elinor Ostrom." *Public Management Review* 16, 3: 299–316.

Allegretti, G., and Herzberg, C. 2004. *Participatory Budgets in Europe. Between Efficiency and Growing Local Democracy*. Tni Briefing Series, No 2004/5, 1–24. TRANSNATIONAL TRANSNATIONAL INSTITUTE and the Centre for Democratic Policy-Making, Amsterdam.

Antiroikko, A.V., Bailey, S.J., Valkama, P. 2011. "Innovations in public governance in the western world." In *Innovations in Public Governance*, edited by Antiroikko, A.V., Bailey, S.J., Valkama, P., 1–22. IOS Press.

Arnstein, S.R. 1969. "A ladder of citizen participation." *Journal of the American Institute of Planners* 35, 4: 216–224.

Barbera, C., Sicilia, M., and Steccolini, I. 2016. "What Mr. Rossi wants in participatory budgeting: two R's (responsiveness and representation) and two I's (inclusiveness and interaction)." *International Journal of Public Administration* 39, 13: 1088–1100.

Bartocci, L., Ebdon, C., Grossi, G., Mauro, S.G. 2021. "The journey of participatory budgeting: A multi-disciplinary literature review." *Working Paper*.

Bartocci, L., Grossi, G., and Mauro, S.G. 2019. "Towards a hybrid logic of participatory budgeting." *International Journal of Public Sector Management* 32, 1: 65–79.

Bartocci, L., Grossi, G., Natalizi, D., and Romizi, S. 2016. "Lo stato dell'arte del bilancio partecipativo in Italia." *Azienda Pubblica* 29, 1: 37–58.

Bassoli, M. 2012. "Participatory budgeting in Italy: An analysis of (almost democratic) participatory governance arrangements." *International Journal of Urban & Regional Research 36*, 6:1183–1203.

Beckett, J., and King, C.S. 2002. "The challenge to improve citizen participation in public budgeting: A discussion." *Journal of Public Budgeting, Accounting & Financial Management 14*, 3: 463.

Berner, M.M., Amos, J.M., and Morse R.S. 2011. "What constitutes effective citizen participation in local government? Views from city stakeholders". *Public Administration Quarterly* 35, 1: 128–163.

Besley, T., and Ghatak, M. 2003. "Incentives, choice, and accountability in the provision of public services." *Oxford Review of Economic Policy* 19, 2: 235–249.

Bingham, L.B., Nabatchi, T., and O'Leary, R. 2005. "The new governance: Practices and processes for stakeholder and citizen participation in the work of government." *Public Administration Review* 65, 5: 547–558.

Bobbio, L. 2019. "Designing effective public participation." *Policy & Society* 38, 1: 41–57.

Bovaird, T. 2005. "Public governance: Balancing stakeholder power in a network society." *International Review of Administrative Sciences* 71, 2: 217–228.

Bovaird, T. 2007. "Beyond engagement and participation: User and community coproduction of public services." *Public Administration Review* 67, 5: 846–860.

Boyle, D., and Harris, M. 2009. *The Challenge of Co-production*, 56. New Economics Foundation.

Brandsen, T., and Honingh, M. 2016. "Distinguishing different types of coproduction: A conceptual analysis based on the classical definitions." *Public Administration Review* 76, 3: 427–435.

Brandsen, T., and Pestoff, V. 2006. "Co-production, the third sector and the delivery of public services: An introduction." *Public Management Review* 8, 4: 493–501.

Brown, J., and Dillard, J. 2015. "Dialogic accountings for stakeholders: On opening up and closing down participatory governance." *Journal of Management Studies* 52, 7: 961–985.

Brudney, J.L., and England, R. 1983. "Towards a definition of the co-production concept." *Public Administration Review* 43, 1: 59–65.

Brun-Martos, M.I., and Lapsley, I. 2017. "Democracy, governmentality and transparency: Participatory budgeting in action." *Public Management Review* 19, 7:1006–1021.

Cabannes, Y., and Lipietz, B. 2018. "Revisiting the democratic promise of participatory budgeting in light of competing political, good governance and technocratic logics." *Environment and Urbanization* 30, 1: 67–84.

Campanale, C., Cinquini, L. and Grossi, G. 2020. "Multiplicity of values in measuring performance of hybrids." In *Hybrid Governance, Organisations and Society: Value Creation Perspectives*, edited by Vakkuri, J. and Johanson, J-E. Routledge.

Campanale, C., Mauro, S.G., and Sancino, A. 2021. "Managing co-production and enhancing good governance principles: insights from two case studies." *Journal of Management and Governance* 25: 275–306.

Célérier, L., and Botey, L.E.C. 2015. "Participatory budgeting at a community level in Porto Alegre: a Bourdieusian interpretation." *Accounting, Auditing & Accountability Journal* 28, 5: 739–772.

Cepiku, D., Marsilio, M., Sicilia, M., and Vainieri, M. 2020. *The Co-production of Public Services*. Palgrave Macmillan.

Cepiku, D., Mussari, R., Poggesi, S., and Reichard, C. 2014. "Special Issue on Governance of networks: challenges and future issues from a public management perspective Editorial." *Journal of Management & Governance* 18, 1: 1–7.

Cinquini, L., Campanale, C., Grossi, G., Mauro, S.G., and Sancino, A. 2017. "Co-production and Governance." In *Global Encyclopedia of Public*

Administration, Public Policy, and Governance, edited by Ali Farazmand, 1–8. Springer International.

Cluley, V., Parker, S. and Radnor, Z. 2020. "New development: Expanding public service value to include dis/value." *Public Money & Management*: 1–4. DOI: 10.1080/09540962.2020.1737392.

Ebdon, C., and Franklin, A. 2004. "Searching for a role for citizens in the budget process." *Public Budgeting & Finance* 24, 1: 32–49.

Ebdon, C., and Franklin, A.L. 2006. "Citizen participation in budgeting theory." *Public Administration Review* 66, 3: 437–447.

European Commission. 2018. *Co-production. Enhancing the role of citizens in governance and service delivery. Technical Dossier*, 4: 1–25.

Fledderus, J. 2015. "Building trust through public service co-production." *International Journal of Public Sector Management* 28, 7: 550–565.

Fung, A. 2006. "Varieties of participation in complex governance." *Public administration review* 66: 66–75.

Fung, A., and Wright, E.O. 2001. "Deepening democracy: Innovations in empowered participatory governance." *Politics & Society* 29, 1: 5–41.

Ganuza, E., and Baiocchi, G. 2012. "The power of ambiguity: How participatory budgeting travels the globe." *Journal of Public Deliberation* 8: 2.

Garlatti, A. et al. 2020. "Co-production and cost efficiency: a structured literature review." *Journal of Public Budgeting, Accounting & Financial Management* 32, 1: 114–135.

Grossi, G., and Thomasson, A. 2015. "Bridging the accountability gap in hybrid organizations: the case of Copenhagen Malmö Port." *International Review of Administrative Sciences* 81, 3: 604–620.

Hartley, J. 2005. "Innovation in governance and public services: Past and present." *Public Money & Management* 25, 1: 27–34.

Jakobsen, M., and Andersen, S. C. 2013. "Coproduction and equity in public service delivery." *Public Administration Review* 73, 5: 704–713.

Lerner, J. 2011. "Participatory budgeting: Building community agreement around tough budget decisions." *National Civic Review* 100, 2: 30–35.

Levine, C.H., and Fisher, G. 1984. "Citizenship and service delivery: The promise of coproduction." *Public Administration Review* 44:178–189.

Manes Rossi, F., and Aversano, N. 2015. "Partecipazione democratica: quale ruolo per la trasparenza? Un'analisi dei siti web dei comuni italiani." *Azienda Pubblica* 2: 121–135.

Mauro, S.G., Rainero, C., and Culasso, F. 2020. "Participatory budgeting: A dialogue among whom?" *Azienda Pubblica* 3: 225–245.

Meijer, A. 2016. "Coproduction as a structural transformation of the public sector." *International Journal of Public Sector Management* 29, 6: 596–611.

Metcalfe, L., and Lapenta, A. 2014. "Partnerships as strategic choices in public management." *Journal of Management & Governance* 18, 1: 51–76.

Michels, A. 2011. "Innovations in democratic governance: How does citizen participation contribute to a better democracy?." *International Review of Administrative Sciences* 77, 2: 275–293.

Nabatchi, T., Sancino, A., and Sicilia, M. 2017. "Varieties of participation in public services: The who, when, and what of coproduction." *Public Administration Review* 77, 5: 766–776.

Needham, C. 2008. "Realising the potential of co-production: Negotiating improvements in public services." *Social Policy & Society* 7, 2: 221–231.

OECD. 2011. *Together for Better Public Services: Partnering with Citizens and Civil Society*. OECD Publishing.

Osborne, S.P. 2006. "The new public governance?" *Public Management Review* 8, 3: 377–387.

Osborne, S.P., and Strokosch, K. 2013. "It takes two to tango? Understanding the c o-production of public services by integrating the services management and public administration perspectives." *British Journal of Management*, 24: S31–S47.

Ostrom, E. 1996. "Crossing the great divide: Coproduction, synergy, and development." *World Development* 24, 6: 1073–1087.

Ottmann, G., Laragy, C., Allen, J., and Feldman, P. 2011. "Coproduction in practice: participatory action research to develop a model of community aged care." *Systemic Practice & Action Research* 24,5: 413–427.

Pestoff, V. 2018. *Co-Production and Public Service Management: Citizenship, Governance and Public Services Management*. Routledge

Poocharoen, O., and Ting, B. 2015. "Collaboration, co-production, networks: Convergence of theories." *Public Management Review* 17, 4: 587–614.

Rossmann, D., and Shanahan, E. A. 2012. "Defining and achieving normative democratic values in participatory budgeting processes." *Public Administration Review* 72, 1: 56–66.

Rubin, M.M., and Ebdon, C. 2020. "Participatory budgeting: Direct democracy in action." *Chinese Public Administration Review* 11, 1: 1–5.

Russo, S. 2013. "Public governance e partecipazione dei cittadini al processo allocativo dei Comuni." *Azienda Pubblica* 1: 61–88.

Sancino, A. 2016. "The meta coproduction of community outcomes: Towards a citizens' capabilities approach." *Voluntas: International Journal of Voluntary and NonProfit Organizations* 27, 1: 409–424.

Shah, A. 2007. *Participatory Budgeting*. World Bank.

Shah, A. 2019. *Participating Budgeting. International Bank for Reconstruction and Development*. The World Bank.

Sicilia, M., Sancino, A., Nabatchi, T., and Guarini, E. 2019. "Facilitating co-production in public services: management implications from a systematic literature review." *Public Money & Management* 39, 4: 233–240.

Sintomer, Y., and Allegretti, G. 2009. *I bilanci partecipativi in Europa*. Ediesse.

Sintomer, Y., Herzberg, C., and Rocke, A. 2008. "Participatory budgeting in Europe: potentials and challenges." *International Journal of Urban & Regional Research* 32, 1: 164–178.

Soguel, N., Caperchione, E., and Cohen, S. 2020. "Allocating government budgets according to citizen preferences: A cross-national survey." *Journal of Public Budgeting, Accounting & Financial Management* 32, 3: 487–504.

Sorrentino, M., Guglielmetti, C., Gilardi, S., and Marsilio, M. 2017. "Health care services and the coproduction puzzle: Filling in the blanks." *Administration & Society* 49, 10: 1424–1449.

de Sousa Santos, B., 1998. "Participatory budgeting in Porto Alegre: Toward a redistributive democracy." *Politics & society* 26, 4: 461–510.

Storlazzi, A. 2006. "Verso una governance dei cittadini. Quali le traiettorie di partecipazione innovativa?." *Azienda Pubblica* 4: 505–521.

Tuurnas, S. 2015. "Learning to co-produce? The perspective of public service professionals." *International Journal of Public Sector Management* 28, 7: 583–598.

Tuurnas, S. 2016. "Looking beyond the normative ideals of neighbourhood projects: How to foster co-production?" *International Journal of Public Administration* 39, 13: 1077–1087.

Uddin, S., Gumb, B., and Kasumba, S. 2011. "Trying to operationalise typologies of the spectacle: A literature review and a case study." *Accounting, Auditing & Accountability Journal* 24, 3: 288–314.

Uddin, S., Mori, Y., Adhikari, P. 2017. "Participatory budgeting in a local government in a vertical society: a Japanese story." *International Review of Administrative Sciences* 85, 3: 490–505.

Verschuere, B., Brandsen, T., and Pestoff, V. 2012. "Co-production: The state of the art in research and the future agenda." *Voluntas: International Journal of Voluntary and Nonprofit Organizations* 23, 4: 1083–1101.

Voorberg, W.H., Bekkers, V.J., and Tummers, L.G. 2015. "A systematic review of co-creation and co-production: Embarking on the social innovation journey." *Public Management Review* 17, 9: 1333–1357.

Wampler, B. 2000. "Orcamento partecipativo: i paradossi della partecipazione a Recife", *Azienda Pubblica*, 13, 6: 751–774.

Wampler, B. 2010. *Participatory Budgeting in Brazil: Contestation, Cooperation, and Accountability*. Penn State Press.

Xavier, J.A., and Bianchi, C. 2020. "An outcome-based dynamic performance management approach to collaborative governance in crime control: insights from Malaysia." *Journal of Management & Governance* 24, 4: 1089–1114.

Yang, K., and Callahan, K. 2007. "Citizen involvement efforts and bureaucratic responsiveness: Participatory values, stakeholder pressures, and administrative practicality." *Public Administration Review* 67, 2: 249–264.

5   Conclusions

5.1 NPM, NPG, and PV: A needed co-existence?

The reform process of the public sector has been the subject of study and debate among public administration, public sector management, and accounting scholars. One source for change has been represented by administrative paradigms (Polzer et al. 2016), such as NPM, NPG, and PV. Although the academic debate has also illustrated other paradigms as the Neo-Weberian State or the Communitarian regime (Pestoff 2018; Pollitt and Bouckaert 2011), NPM, NPG, and PV are included in the current analysis since they have become well known and popular worldwide, inspiring the introduction of several practices in public sector organizations. On the one hand, paradigms and reform trajectories can provide an approximate and simplified representation of different scenarios across countries. On the other hand, they are useful in explaining reform trends and reflecting on underlying belief systems.

As discussed in the previous chapters (in particular, Chapters 1 and 3), NPM and NPG have been seen as dominant paradigms, and they are characterized by specific ideas, priorities, and 'solutions' to be adopted. More recently, the PV approach has attracted the attention of scholars. Each of these paradigms can be considered the expression of a specific logic, such as market capitalism for NPM and democracy for NPG (Polzer et al. 2016). PV emphasizes the ultimate goal of government activities, namely value creation. The differences among the paradigms are thus visible, although the relationship between them is ambiguous and complex (Stoker 2006).

Generally, NPM, NPG, and PV have been considered reform paradigms that have followed each other over time. From this perspective, they are consequent paradigms, given that each reform paradigm can be considered a response or reaction to the previous one, with new reforms being interpreted as a potential means to address the challenges and limitations of previous reforms. According to this view, NPM has been considered a reaction to the public administration (PA) paradigm, which has itself been criticized for being unsuitable for improving efficiency and effectiveness due to its excessive focus on compliance, control of inputs, and hierarchical command. NPM has thus been predominantly linked to the measurement and audit of performance, the search for efficiency and effectiveness and not only for the economy, and the institutional re-organization of public sector organizations by means of delegation, privatization, and agencification. NPM has emphasized the power of the market and has interpreted citizens as clients/consumers (Ackerman 2004; Lapsley 2008). From this perspective, NPM can be considered the movement that has supported the search for an efficient state. However, it has not been free of challenges and limitations, and a significant debate has been nurtured on its limits. For instance, the strong emphasis on competition and market powers may fail in considering that competition can be absent in the public sector, and the specification and monitoring of outputs may prove to be difficult, with the added consequence of delivering poor services at high costs (Alford and Hughes 2008).

NPG has become prominent in such discussions. Compared to NPM, NPG maintains that the delivery of public services should be managed in a collaborative way in order to increase responsiveness to citizens' needs and effectiveness. The trust in the market inspired by NPM has here been replaced by the trust in the power of collaborations. Indeed, NPG is characterized by its focus on networks, collaborative and participatory governance mechanisms, and the search for effectiveness. This perspective, focused on public governance, has pushed the creation of a new model of a participatory state through collaboration among internal and external stakeholders (Meneguzzo and Cepiku 2006). In line with what has been labelled as NPG, PV has emphasized the relevance of focusing on the services to deliver and the value to create. After the post-bureaucratic paradigm of NPM, PV marks the turn of a post-competitive paradigm (O'Flynn 2007): Public managers are required to collaborate, communicate, and coordinate with many actors to produce public value, while according to NPM, they were expected to focus on efficiency rather than value creation (O'Flynn 2007). PV emphasizes public value and values, with a recognition of the relevance of citizenship as well as democratic and collaborative governance.

Nevertheless, the transition among movements is not a linear process (Christensen 2012; Iacovino et al. 2017). Indeed, the previous clear-cut distinction among paradigms and their temporal sequence does not necessarily find support in practice. According to an alternative view, the three paradigms can be considered as potential parallel paradigms that co-exist. The co-existence can occur in different ways. Indeed, while existing practices can be replaced by new ones, they can also be partially revised and modified. Paradigms can be combined with each other, resulting in hybrid practices and belief systems. Transitional combinations or more permanent forms of hybridity can be detected in practice (Polzer et al. 2016). Various elements of different paradigms can be added on top of each other, such that the components of each paradigm are still identifiable (layering), or the various elements can be mixed to result in a new paradigm, which has also been referred to as blending (Polzer et al. 2016). Previous scholars have also talked of sedimentation to refer to the fact that new ideas àre added to existing ones (Hyndman et al. 2014; Pollitt and Bouckaert 2011). Accordingly, 'sedimentation reflects a slow, layered, dialectical pattern of elements of new emerging structures, systems and beliefs combined with pre-existing ones' (Hyndman et al. 2014, 402). Therefore, since different administrative paradigms can be combined, hybridization is a possibility (Polzer et al. 2016).

Hybridity and hybridization are ambiguous terms that are defined differently in the literature. Their conceptual investigation is beyond the scope of this chapter. In a broad view, hybrid can be associated with what is produced by two or more elements that are usually found separately (Miller et al. 2008), and a hybrid organisation can comprise public and private actors providing public services for citizens (Johanson and Vakkuri 2017; Vakkuri and Johanson 2020). A hybrid organization can also be identified in terms of outputs produced, ownership, funding, and governance structure. Scholars also talk about the hybridization of governance logics to explain the shift from one logic to another (e.g. from NPM to NPG), in which case hybridization is defined as the process through which elements of different logics are integrated (Wiesel and Modell 2014). Empirical studies support the thesis that elements of different paradigms can be identified in the same context and reflected in the adoption of different reforms (Hyndman et al. 2014; Polzer et al. 2016).

These perspectives reveal the complexity of reform processes that do not follow a linear path and assume different characteristics even according to the scenario. Indeed, one way to explain the different reforms adopted by countries and the variation within the same country concerning how reforms are designed and implemented is related to the particular institutional arrangements and cultural and administrative styles (Ongaro 2009; Painter and Peters 2010). In this regard, for instance, performance regimes (Talbot 2010) are considered a combination of the institutional context and performance interventions, which are the actions taken by institutional actors.

5.1.1 A focus on performance and budgeting

Although performance is not a new issue that public organizations are required to deal with, and the improvement of performance is an old desire, the interpretation of performance has changed significantly with the advent of NPM and in the post-NPM era. It is not frozen in time (Schick 2003). Defining the meaning of performance and being able to measure and manage it have proven to be significant challenges for public sector organizations. According to Dubnick (2005), 'The word performance is both blessed and cursed by its synonymic nature' (391). If a most basic and simpler form of performance focuses on the tasks to be carried out, a more advanced approach pays more attention to the quality of the results produced. In the spirit of NPM, significant attention has been paid to quantifying efficiency and effectiveness. Then, the widening of governance arrangements, the growing relevance of collaborations and networks, and the increasingly important role of citizens have contributed to increasing the emphasis on different forms of measuring and managing performance. Compared to the focus on compliance with rules and regulations of PA, the key aspects of performance under NPM concern efficiency and financial results, while under NPG and PV, effectiveness and citizen/customer satisfaction assume more importance (Wiesel and Modell 2014), despite the difficulties in measuring outcome and effectiveness. The objectives shift from economy, efficiency, and effectiveness to satisfaction, outcomes, and trust (O'Flynn 2007). Accordingly, the types of performance measures and indicators differ, as do the design and use of performance information systems (van Helden et al. 2012). Empirical studies have demonstrated that performance measurement and management systems designed according to the NPM paradigm may require revision and adaptation if applied to the context of hybrid settings and inter-organizational relationships (Agostino and Arnaboldi 2015; Rajala et al. 2020). In this case, there is a call for consideration of the role of different actors in the design and delivery of services in order to monitor and account for their performance while also including them in the design of the performance measures (Agostino and Arnablodi 2015; Campanale et al. 2021).

In addition to influencing the object of performance, these paradigms have affected the identification of the performing agency and of the accountability mechanisms (see Box 5.1 for an overview on accountability). Recognizing who is the performing agent in charge of achieving a specific goal and who is being made accountable for the results achieved becomes more difficult when the boundaries of the public sector are blurred and multiple actors are involved in the design and delivery of public value.

In the NPM era, high trust in the market has influenced the concept of public accountability, thereby establishing its foundation on audit and reporting activities (Almqvist et al. 2013) and emphasizing hierarchical relationships. The vertical performance of single organizations has been a key concern. Performance-based accountability has been developed and reflected in several tools and performance interventions, such as performance budgets. In the NPG era, the extension of actors involved in public service delivery and the redesign of boundaries have shaped management control, leading to increased dimensions to control and the broadening of the number and type of indicators to be considered. Under NPG, the view of citizens changes and shifts from considering them as consumers to empowering them and viewing them as co-producers (Bovaird 2007; Wiesel and Modell 2014). Unlike NPM, NPG recognizes horizontal relationships (Klijn 2012), and this inclination is linked to different accountability mechanisms involving social and moral obligations according to which the different organizations that collaborate to provide services perceive the obligation to report their activities and/or results (Hodges 2012). With NPG and PV, the approach to accountability becomes increasingly multifaceted.

BOX 5.1: INSIGHTS INTO ACCOUNTABILITY

Accountability in the public sector can mean several things. It is an elusive term that is subjectively constructed (Sinclair 1995). According to the definition provided by Barton (2006), 'accountability involves an obligation to answer for one's decisions and actions when authority to act on behalf of one party (the principal) is transferred to another (the agent)' (257). This obligation in the public sector arises since citizens delegate the use of their resources and the related decision-making powers to the government, which is in charge of formulating and implementing public policies. Consequently, the government has the obligation to act on behalf and in the interest of the citizens, accounting for what the government does and how this is done. This is also known as the political side of accountability. In addition, it is possible to identify a second form of accountability, which can be defined as a 'managerial' form that concerns the relationships between politicians and managers. According to this latter type of accountability, managers should account to politicians for how they fulfil their tasks and use the allocated resources. Political and managerial forms of accountability (Broadbent and Laughlin 2003) have been integrated by multiple conceptualizations and classifications of accountability mechanisms. Political, managerial, but also public, professional, and personal forms of accountability have been identified (Sinclair 1995). The chain of accountability may be complicated and made up of multiple layers as it accounts for not only citizens, parliament, and governments, but also other actors, such as public–private partnerships, third-sector organizations, networks, and hybrid organizations (Barton 2006). Indeed, accountability mechanisms can change from vertical forms that link principal and agent to horizontal mechanisms that link different actors engaged in the delivery of services (Grossi and Thomasson 2015). In addition to the variation due to the actors involved, accountability may also have a different 'object'. This implies that actors may have to account for the appropriate use of resources according to the law, or for the results obtained, thus inspiring performance-based accountability (Dubnick 2005; Monteduro 2012). Nevertheless, the attempt at improving performance through accountability may have the opposite effects (Dubnick 2005), emphasizing the ambiguity and challenging nature of accountability mechanisms.

The changing conceptualization and role of accountability are also visible in budgeting reforms. Budgeting features and its different roles have been redefined over time and still need to be investigated (Anessi-Pessina et al. 2016). During the 1980s, budgeting reforms were driven by the call for controlling public expenditures, increasing efficiency and effectiveness, and responding to changing needs. To address the multiple expectations built on budgeting, its reforms have been increasingly linked to changes in planning and performance measurement and management systems (Pollitt and Bouckaert 2004). These changes appear to have been aligned with NPM reforms.

Despite not being the first attempt, NPM has introduced elements of performance measurement and management in public budgeting to support rational decision-making. The budgeting reforms relating to performance have changed over time, influencing the format and content of the budgets, the documents, or the procedures (Pollitt and Bouckaert 2011). With NPM, the focus has shifted from legal to performance control and performance-based accountability. The political function traditionally investigated to a greater extent has been combined with an enriched managerial function in the NPM era (Saliterer et al. 2017). However, the focus on performance has been limited by the practical difficulties in measuring performance. The complexities of the tasks and roles of public sector organizations and their complex organization are not aligned with simple conceptualizations that tend to consider outputs and processes homogeneous (ter Bogt et al. 2015). In these regards, it has interestingly been noted that it is not possible to account for several activities being performed in collaboration with other organizations and actors. Designing performance budgeting should take into explicit account the relevance of collaborations.

Old questions are again actual. Is PBB useful for public sector organizations in coping with the current problems? Or is it only 'old wine in a new bottle' (Martin 1997)? Is it destined to fail again, as in the past, while the traditional budget will last (Wildavsky 1978)? The experiences with PBB and the widespread difficulties in implementing it have shown the existence of a gap between promises and practices. As recent studies have pointed out, on the one hand, PBB confirms itself as a praiseworthy attempt to focus on what public sector organizations have to achieve with public resources. On the other hand, the reform of performance budgeting requires an incremental approach whereby improvements are made in a continuous and constant learning process, with reform being used as a tool for achieving different purposes. It is important to adapt the practice to the context and focus on the use of performance data as an interim measure of progress (Kroll 2015). These reforms are still on the agenda of many public sector organizations, despite the development of further reforms. The changing role of governments and the increasing involvement of citizens have resulted in the revitalization of participatory budgeting, which appears in line with NPG and at the same time can be designed and implemented in the spirit of different paradigms and logics (Pestoff 2018).

This has moved us to reflect on the need for an integration of different tools and paradigms in a comprehensive and integrative framework. As shown by previous research, the application of a reform such as PBB does not necessarily replace previous reforms, signalling the tensions existing among paradigms (Grossi et al. 2018). The adoption of PBB may coexist with traditional budgeting approaches inspired by different paradigms as well as participatory budgeting can rely on bureaucratic and NPM ideas to be successful, contrary to the expectations (Aleksandrov and Timoshenko 2018). Accordingly, the evidence – reported in the previous chapters – on the limitations and challenges of the budgeting reforms adopted over time by governments pave the way for reflecting on the need of integrating different reforms and paradigms rather than focusing on their exclusive selection. In this regard, as recently recognized (Steccolini 2019), it can be important to reflect more on the concept of publicness to guide public sector reform and rethink the role of accounting and accountability.

5.2 What's next?

Natural disasters, economic and financial crises, and inequalities and difficulties in the health care and education systems are examples of factors that have impacted the agendas of the public, private, and third sectors in recent times (Bryson et al. 2014). In particular, one of the most recent events to have impacted the worldwide economy and society is the new global pandemic of COVID-19, which has challenged governments in both developing and developed countries. The spread of the virus has been acknowledged since the beginning of 2020, and its persistence led the World Health Organization to declare a global pandemic in March. Consequently, public and private health systems, national economies, and exchanges across countries have been significantly affected.

According to the OECD Secretary-General, the economic shock produced by the virus has been bigger than that of the previous global financial crisis (Grossi et al. 2020). The measures taken by governments to deal with the shock in the short term have differed from one country to another and will have significant budgetary implications in the long term (Grossi et al. 2020). Governments will likely have to face higher government deficits and debts in the future.

Regardless of the current state of uncertainty, the pandemic offers important opportunities for reflection. In these complex times, budgeting reveals its relevant and challenging nature. The allocative decisions concerning the number of resources to be used and the purpose of their use, which have been historically difficult decisions, have become even more difficult in this period. Indeed, the COVID-19 pandemic has shown how difficult it can be to determine which types of resources are needed, decide how to use them, and define the priority of the different goals contributing to society's financial and social sustainability (e.g. Schick 2003; Wildavsky 1978). Re-budgeting, which indicates the possibility of revising the budget during the financial year, plays an even more important role during the COVID-19 crisis (Anessi-Pessina et al. 2020) as it allows for intervention and revision of previous decisions according to the details of the emerging scenario.

However, the possibility of revision does not itself result in easy-to-make choices. The pandemic has highlighted how budgetary decisions are determined by multiple and sometimes conflictual values and goals: On the one hand, the pursuit of health-related concerns is essential in order to save human lives; on the other hand, the economic and financial concerns about the production activities in each sector of the economy are also important, as are concerns about public services, such as education. The politics of budgeting become more complex in order to manage the interests of the different parties involved in a context of uncertainties.

In the previous chapters, it has already been shown how problematic and ambiguous budgeting can be. Problems and ambiguities are exacerbated in times of crisis. During these times, it becomes even more difficult to have the required understanding of the scenario in order to make proper decisions. Indeed, countries all over the world have made different decisions to cope with the pandemic based on their different understandings of the circumstances (Nørreklit et al. 2021). For instance, Finland and Norway considered the pandemic to be a serious threat to the country, while Sweden has treated COVID-19 as a difficult flu, with severe effects on budgetary decisions (Argento et al. 2020). The recognition of the severity of COVID-19 was different across countries and the consequent uncertainty complicated action choices and influenced the results in the management of the crisis, as shown by the comparative analysis of Germany, Italy, and the UK (Nørreklit et al. 2021).

In this context, allocative decisions are difficult. They may need to consider the objectives to be reached (future performance) rather than past results (past performance). The elaboration of the goals to achieve and the definition of the objectives for the future can guide the allocation and management of resources and contribute to control over the resources. A clear strategy is thus extremely important to inspire sound budgetary decisions (Argento et al. 2020). During the COVID-19 crisis, such strategic decision-making has been challenged by the contested understanding of the scenario and the contested idea of public value(s). Thus, we are left asking the following questions: What should be created? What values should be prioritized?

In the case of COVID-19, one mechanism put in place by governments to handle the crisis has been the involvement of citizens. According to the Italian experience, citizens have been engaged not in budgeting decision-making (participatory budgeting) but in alternative participatory mechanisms. Citizens have been asked to provide information on their health and their movements (*information sharing*), to stay at home, wear masks when out, and apply social distancing (*individual actions*), thus contributing to the avoidance of disvalue. At the same time, they have been involved in the creation of value co-delivering services, as shown by parents' involvement in online educational services (*co-produced actions*) (Anessi-Pessina et al. 2020). The Council of Europe has published several recommendations for maintaining and improving citizens' engagement during the COVID-19 restrictions.

At this moment, the crisis is not yet over, and governments worldwide are struggling to cope with it; it is therefore not possible to make any final statements on the effects of the budgetary decisions made and their consequences on the performance of governments. However, it is possible to reflect on the current events and develop some insights. First, deciding how to allocate the available resources to the different budget programmes requires a plan of action and a strategy that is clear, shared, and transparent, with a view of the long-term implications. Flexibility and strategic orientation are pivotal. It will be important to identify the key strategic objectives and values that will receive more attention in the future (Grossi et al. 2020). From this perspective, it is evident that performance, in terms of future results to achieve, and values, in terms of values to realize, can play a role to influence the allocation and management of resources.

Second, the crucial role that citizens can play in the delivery and creation of value has been clear during the crisis. This suggests that future reforms should continue to attend to how citizens can become engaged in the decision-making process.

Third, the growth of the digital transformation of public service delivery (Agostino et al. 2021) may support the next stage of reforms, and such changes call for proper consideration and use by governments. The call for their proper use takes place in an era characterized by digitalization of the language which is changing governance, accounting, and performance management of organizations and where the use of digital tools is often uncritical (Cinquini 2019).

As shown by these brief considerations, it may be important to integrate different reforms and approaches to cope with the current crisis.

The past decades have seen the development of continuous budgeting reforms. Those managerial reforms strengthening performance measurement and management and adopting a performance-oriented approach to budgeting are still alive, despite the need for improvement. The managerial accountability orientation strongly introduced in the 1980s has now to cope with a different scenario characterized by the spread of inter-organizational arrangements, hybrid organizations, collaborative mechanisms, and the co-production of services. Accordingly, the conceptualization, measurement, and management of performance have changed, and the public budget has undertaken further revisions that have paved the way for the development of participatory approaches to public budgeting. However, the reforms have proven to not be exclusive, and they can co-exist and mutually influence each other. There is neither a one-best-way paradigm nor a one-best-way reform. The design of the reforms should respond to the specific needs of the context. Accordingly, the greater challenges come from the changes in the external context. The current scenario demonstrates how the public budget may struggle to perform in cases of crisis, uncertainty, and emergency. Therefore, it will be interesting and relevant to observe the revisions of public budgeting and performance to respond to the changing political, economic, and social needs, their effects, and which, if any, paradigms will be dominant in leading the next wave of reforms. A crisis can change or confirm the current paradigmatic approach to reform (Mussari et al. 2020). Future research on budgeting, accounting, and performance management will help to improve understanding of the effects of the decisions made during the pandemic as well as how the crisis has influenced budgetary decision-making and consequently the performance of governments. It will be important to further investigate the role of accounting and accountability in the contemporary scenario and in light of the new challenges to public services and values.

References

Ackerman, J. 2004. "Co-governance for accountability: Beyond "exit" and "voice"." *World Development* 32, 3: 447–463.

Agostino, D., and Arnaboldi, M. 2015. "The new public management in hybrid settings: New challenges for performance measures." *International Review of Public Administration* 20, 4: 353–369.

Agostino, D., Arnaboldi, M., and Lema, M.D. 2021. "New development: COVID-19 as an accelerator of digital transformation in public service delivery." *Public Money & Management* 41, 1: 69–72.

Aleksandrov, E., and Timoshenko, K., 2018. "Translating participatory budgeting in Russia: The roles of inscriptions and inscriptors." *Journal of Accounting in Emerging Economies* 8, 3.

Alford, J., and Hughes, O. 2008. "Public value pragmatism as the next phase of public management." *The American Review of Public Administration* 38, 2: 130–148.

Almqvist, R., Grossi, G., van Helden, G.J., and Reichard, C. 2013. "Public sector governance and accountability." *Critical Perspectives on Accounting* 24, 7–8: 479–487.

Anessi-Pessina, E., Barbera, C., Langella, C., Manes-Rossi, F., Sancino, A., Sicilia, M., and Steccolini, I. 2020. "Reconsidering public budgeting after the COVID-19 outbreak: Key lessons and future challenges." *Journal of Public Budgeting, Accounting & Financial Management.*

Anessi-Pessina, E., Barbera, C., Sicilia, M., and Steccolini, I. 2016. "Public sector budgeting: A European review of accounting and public management journals." *Accounting, Auditing & Accountability Journal* 29, 3: 491–519.

Argento, D., Kaarbøe, K., and Vakkuri, J. 2020. "Constructing certainty through public budgeting: Budgetary responses to the COVID-19 pandemic in Finland, Norway and Sweden." *Journal of Public Budgeting, Accounting & Financial Management.*

Barton, A.D. 2006. "Public sector accountability and commercial-in-confidence outsourcing contracts." *Accounting, Auditing & Accountability Journal* 19, 2: 256–271.

ter Bogt, H.J., Helden, G.J., and Kolk, B. 2015. "Challenging the NPM ideas about performance management: Selectivity and differentiation in outcome-oriented performance budgeting." *Financial Accountability and Management* 31, 3: 287–315.

Bovaird, T. 2007. "Beyond engagement and participation: User and community coproduction of public services." *Public Administration Review* 67, 5: 846–860.

Broadbent, J., and Laughlin, R. 2003. "Control and legitimation in government accountability processes: The private finance initiative in the UK." *Critical Perspectives on Accounting* 14, 1–2: 23–48.

Bryson, J.M., Crosby, B.C., and Bloomberg, L. 2014. "Public value governance: Moving beyond traditional public administration and the new public management." *Public Administration Review* 74, 4: 445–456.

Campanale, C., Mauro, S.G., and Sancino, A. 2021. "Managing co-production and enhancing good governance principles: insights from two case studies." *Journal of Management and Governance* 25: 275–306.

Christensen, T. 2012. "Post-NPM and changing public governance." *Journal of Political Science & Economics* 1, 1: 1–11.

Cinquini, L. 2019. "Editorial: JMG Symposium on "evaluation, performance and governance in the digital age." *Journal of Management & Governance*, 23(4), pp.847–848.

Dubnick, M. 2005. "Accountability and the promise of performance: In search of the mechanisms." *Public Performance & Management Review* 28, 3: 376–417.

Grossi, G., Ho, A.T., and Joyce, P.G. 2020. "Budgetary responses to a global pandemic: International experiences and lessons for a sustainable future." *Journal of Public Budgeting, Accounting & Financial Management.*

Grossi, G., Mauro, S.G., and Vakkuri, J. 2018. "Converging and diverging pressures in PBB development: the experiences of Finland and Sweden." *Public Management Review* 20, 12: 1836–1857.

Grossi, G., and Thomasson, A. 2015. "Bridging the accountability gap in hybrid organizations: the case of Copenhagen Malmö Port." *International Review of Administrative Sciences* 81, 3: 604–620.

Van Helden, G.J., Johnsen, Å., and Vakkuri, J. 2012. "The life-cycle approach to performance management: Implications for public management and evaluation." *Evaluation* 18, 2: 159–175.

Hodges, R. 2012. "Joined-up government and the challenges to accounting and accountability researchers." *Financial Accountability & Management* 28, 1: 26–51.

Hyndman, N., Liguori, M., Meyer, R.E., Polzer, T., Rota, S., and Seiwald, J. 2014. "The translation and sedimentation of accounting reforms. A comparison of the UK, Austrian and Italian experiences." *Critical Perspectives on Accounting* 25, 4–5: 388–408.

Iacovino, N.M., Barsanti, S., and Cinquini, L. 2017. "Public organizations between old public administration, new public management and public governance: the case of the Tuscany region." *Public Organization Review* 17, 1: 61–82.

Johanson, J.E., and Vakkuri, J. 2017. *Governing Hybrid Organisations: Exploring Diversity of Institutional Life.* Routledge.

Klijn, E.H. 2012. "New public management and governance: A comparison." *Oxford Handbook of Governance*, edited by Levi- Faur, 201–214. Oxford University Press.

Kroll, A. 2015. "Drivers of performance information use: Systematic literature review and directions for future research." *Public Performance & Management Review* 38, 3: 459–486.

Lapsley, I. 2008. "The NPM agenda: back to the future." *Financial Accountability & Management* 24, 1: 77–96.

Martin, L.L. 1997. "Outcome budgeting: A new entrepreneural approach to budgeting." *Journal of Public Budgeting, Accounting & Financial Management* 9, 1: 108.

Meneguzzo, M., and Cepiku, D. 2006. "La public governance: Quadro concettuale di riferimento, confronto internazionale e specificità della situazione italiana". In *Studi sulla governance delle aziende*, edited by Abatecola, G., and Poggesi, S., 89–111. Giappichelli.

Miller, P., Kurunmäki, L., and O'Leary, T. 2008. "Accounting, hybrids and the management of risk." *Accounting, Organizations & Society* 33, 7–8: 942–967.

Monteduro, F. 2012. *Evoluzione ed effetti dell'accountability nelle amministrazioni pubbliche*. Maggioli Editore.

Mussari, R., Cepiku, D., and Sorrentino, D. 2020. "Governmental accounting reforms at a time of crisis: The Italian governmental accounting harmonization." *Journal of Public Budgeting, Accounting & Financial Management*.

Nørreklit, H. et al. 2021. "Evaluating performance management of COVID-19 reality in three European countries: A pragmatic constructivist study." *Accounting, Auditing & Accountability Journal*. DOI: 10.1108/AAAJ-08-2020-4778.

O'Flynn, J. 2007. "From new public management to public value: Paradigmatic change and managerial implications." *Australian Journal of Public Administration* 66, 3: 353–366.

Ongaro, E. 2009. *Public Management Reform and Modernization: Trajectories of Administrative Change in Italy, France, Greece, Portugal and Spain*. Edward Elgar Publishing.

Painter, M., and Peters, B.G., 2010. "The analysis of administrative traditions." In *Tradition and Public Administration*, edited by Painter, M., and Peters, B. G., 3–16. Palgrave Macmillan.

Pestoff, V. 2018. *Co-production and Public Service Management: Citizenship, Governance and Public Services Management*. Routledge.

Pollitt, C., and Bouckaert, G. 2004. *Public Management Reform: A Comparative Analysis*. Oxford University Press.

Pollitt, C., and Bouckaert, G. 2011. *Public Management Reform: A Comparative Analysis of NPM, the Neo-Weberian State, and New Public Governance*. Oxford University Press.

Polzer, T., Meyer, R.E., Höllerer, M.A., and Seiwald, J. 2016. "Institutional hybridity in public sector reform: Replacement, blending, or layering of administrative paradigms". In *How Institutions Matter!*, edited by Gehman, J., Lounsbury, M., and Greenwood, R., 69–99. Emerald Group Publishing Limited.

Rajala, T., Laihonen, H., and Vakkuri, J. 2020. "Exploring challenges of boundary-crossing performance dialogues in hybrids." *Journal of Management & Governance* 24, 3: 799–820.

Saliterer, I., Sicilia, M., and Steccolini, I. 2017. "Public budgets and budgeting: State of the art and future challenges." In *Handbook of Public Administration and Management in Europe*, edited by E. Ongaro and S. Van Thiel, 141–163. Palgrave.

Schick, A. 2003. "The performing state: Reflection on an idea whose time has come but whose implementation has not." *OECD Journal on Budgeting* 3, 2: 71–103.

Sinclair, A. 1995. "The chameleon of accountability: forms and discourses." *Accounting, Organizations and Society* 20, 2/3: 219–237.

Steccolini, I. 2019. "Accounting and the post-new public management." *Accounting, Auditing & Accountability Journal* 32, 1: 255–279.

Stoker, G. 2006. "Public value management: a new narrative for networked governance?" *The American review of public administration* 36, 1: 41–57.

Talbot, C. 2010. *Theories of Performance: Organizational and Service Improvement in the Public Domain.* Oxford University Press.

Vakkuri, J., and Johanson, J.E. 2020. *Hybrid Governance, Organisations and Society: Value Creation Perspectives.* Routledge.

Wiesel, F., and Modell, S. 2014. "From new public management to new public governance? Hybridization and implications for public sector consumerism." *Financial Accountability & Management* 30, 2:175–205.

Wildavsky, A. 1978. "A budget for all seasons? Why the traditional budget lasts." *Public Administration Review* 38, 6: 501–509.

Index